HOW TO COOK
YOUR FAVOURITE
TAKEAWAYS
AT HOME

Other cookery titles from Spring Hill, an imprint of How To Books:

EVERYDAY COOKING FOR ONE
Imaginative, delicious and healthy recipes that make cooking for one ... fun
Wendy Hobson

THE EVERYDAY FISH COOKBOOK
Simple, delicious recipes for cooking fish
Trish Davies

EVERYDAY THAI COOKING
Easy, authentic recipes from Thailand to cook for friends and family
Siripan Akvanich

THE EVERYDAY HALOGEN FAMILY COOKBOOK
Sarah Flower

MAKE YOUR OWN ORGANIC ICE CREAM
Using home grown and local produce
Ben Vear

HOW TO COOK YOUR FAVOURITE TAKEAWAYS AT HOME
The food you like to eat when you want to eat it – at less cost and with more goodness
Carolyn Humphries

Write or phone for a catalogue to:

How To Books
Spring Hill House
Spring Hill Road
Begbroke
Oxford
OX5 1RX
Tel. 01865 375794

Or email: info@howtobooks.co.uk

Visit our website www.howtobooks.co.uk to find out more about us and our books.

Like our Facebook page How To Books & Spring Hill

Follow us on Twitter @Howtobooksltd

Read our books online www.howto.co.uk

HOW TO COOK
YOUR FAVOURITE
TAKEAWAYS
AT HOME

The food you like to eat when you want to eat it
– at less cost and with more goodness

Carolyn Humphries

SPRING HILL

Published by Spring Hill, an imprint of How To Books Ltd.
Spring Hill House, Spring Hill Road
Begbroke, Oxford OX5 1RX
United Kingdom
Tel: (01865) 375794
Fax: (01865) 379162
info@howtobooks.co.uk
www.howtobooks.co.uk

First published 2012

How To Books greatly reduce the carbon footprint of their books
by sourcing their typesetting and printing in the UK.

British Library Cataloguing in Publication Data
A catalogue record of this book is available from the British Library.

ISBN: 978 1 905862 93 1

Produced for How To Books by Deer Park Productions, Tavistock, Devon
Designed and typeset by Mousemat Design Ltd
Edited by Wendy Hobson
Printed and bound by in Great Britain by Bell & Bain Ltd, Glasgow

NOTE: The material contained in this book is set out in good faith for general
guidance and no liability can be accepted for loss or expense incurred as a
result of relying in particular circumstances on statements made in the book.
Laws and regulations are complex and liable to change, and readers should
check the current position with relevant authorities before making personal
arrangements.

Contents

Introduction   9

1 Your Kitchen   11

2 Notes and Conversion Charts   15

3 From the Curry House   19
Tandoori Chicken   20
Chicken Tikka Masala   21
Quick Chicken Madras   22
Chicken Tikka   23
Quick Prawn Curry   24
Pork Vindaloo   25
Keema Curry with Peas   26
Palak Gosht   27
Lamb Biryani   28
Lamb Rogan Josh   29
Lamb Korma   30
Onion Bhajis   31
Mini Vegetable Samosas   32
Cucumber Raita   34
Sag Aloo   35
Bombay Aloo   36
Mixed Vegetable Curry   37

Instant Dal   38
Masoor Dal   39
Indian Carrot Salad   40
Simple Pilau Rice   41
Baked Vegetable Pilau Rice   42
Quick Naan Bread   43

4 From the Chinese Takeaway   45
Chicken and Sweetcorn Soup   46
Wonton Soup   47
Egg Foo Yung   48
Sweet and Sour Pork   49
Chinese Spare Ribs   50
Chinese Chicken Curry   51
Chicken Chow Mein   52
Peking Duck   53
Beef with Mushrooms and Oyster Sauce 54
Ginger Beef with Mangetout   55
Prawns with Cashew Nuts   56
Prawn Toasts   57
Szechuan Spicy Peanut Noodles with
     Vegetables   58
Egg Fried Rice   59
Quick Vegetable Stir-fry   60

Beansprout and Pepper Salad	61	Double Cheese Burgers	91
Spring Rolls	62	Chicken and Bacon Burgers	92
Crispy Seaweed	63	Sausage Burgers with Mushrooms	
		and Apple	93
5 From the Pizza House	**65**	Veggie Burgers	94
Quick Pan Pizza	66	Fish Fillet Burgers	95
Fast Flatbread Pizza	67	Matchstick French Fries	96
Basic Pizza Dough	68	Root Crisps	97
Pizza Napolitana	69		
Pizza Fiorentina	70	**8 From the Chicken Shack**	**99**
Spicy Meat Feast Pizza	71	Oven-fried Chicken	100
Four Seasons Pizza	72	Savoury-coated Crispy Fried Chicken	101
Deep-pan Filled Crust Pizza	73	Smoky Glazed Chicken Wings	102
Calzone	74	Chicken Nuggets with Barbecue	
What's in My Fridge Stuffed Pizza	75	Dipping Sauce	103
Italian Salad	76	Chilli Chicken Salad Wrap	104
Dough Balls	77	Crispy Fillet Burger	
		with Pepper Mayonnaise	105
6 From the Chippy	**79**	Coleslaw	106
Classic Battered Fish and Chips	80	Fluffy Mash	107
Oven-baked Crumb-coated Fish and Chips	82	Barbecued Beans	108
Quick Fish Cakes	83	Roasted Corn Cobs	109
Pig in a Crispy Blanket	84	Jacket Potatoes with Soured Cream	
Mushy Peas	85	and Chives	110
Easy Pickled Eggs	86	Golden Oven Wedges	111
Quick Tartare Sauce	87		
		9 From the Pie Shop	**113**
7 From the Burger Joint	**89**	Cornish Pasties	114
Classic Hamburgers with All the Trimmings	90	Lamb and Mint Pies with	

Leeks and Carrots	115	Thai-style Crab Cakes	138
Steak and Onion Pasties	116	Thai Chicken Satay with Crunchy	
Steak Guinness and Stilton Pies	117	Peanut Sauce	139
East End-style Pie and Liquor	118	Thai Noodles	140
Chicken and Mushroom Pies	120	Sweet Chilli Dipping Sauce	141
Giant Sausage Rolls	122	Thai Rocket and Cashew Salad	142
Cheese Tomato and Pesto Pies	123	Thai-dressed Green Salad	143

10 From the Kebab House 125

Shish Kebabs 126

Kofta Kebabs 127

Lamb Doner Kebabs 128

Vegetable Shish Kebabs 129

Tzatsiki 130

Village Salad 131

11 From the Thai Takeaway 133

Thai Red Beef Curry 134

Thai Red Vegetable Curry 135

Thai Green Chicken Curry 136

Pad Thai 137

12 From the Japanese Noodle

and Sushi Bar 145

Miso Soup 146

Chicken and Vegetable Rice Noodle Soup 147

Seafood Ramen Noodle Soup 148

Salmon Teryaki 149

Chicken Yakitori 150

Vegetable Tempura 151

Mixed Sushi Platter 152

Japanese-style Mixed Vegetable Salad 154

Japanese Daikon and Carrot Salad 155

Index 156

Introduction

Takeaways are deliciously addictive. When you decide you fancy a curry, Chinese, pizza or good old fish 'n' chips nothing else will do. As you drool over the menu, you conveniently forget that they are full of fat, salt and sugar so are pretty unhealthy *and* they cost a fortune! It's okay if you only have them occasionally, but more and more of us are turning to them on a regular basis because it's the food we love to eat; but the trouble is it's punishing our waistlines and our bank balances!

But now you can have the best of both worlds. In *How to Cook Your Favourite Takeaways at Home* you'll find easy, great-tasting, packed-with-goodness versions of all your favourite fast foods, using simple, fresh and frozen ingredients; plus all the accompaniments you need so you can create sumptuous, well-balanced meals the whole family will enjoy. Many are so quick and easy they make great after-work dinners as they can be thrown together in just a few minutes, others take a little longer to prepare so may be better kept for weekends and special occasions, when you want a whole themed meal, for instance. But you can rest assured that none is complicated and all taste terrific! There are plenty of great tips, too, on how to prepare in advance, what to look out for when shopping, how to cut corners to speed things up, and what to keep in your storecupboard so you can knock up a delicious meal any time. Most are freezable, too, so with one lot of preparation, you can have some meals stashed away ready to grab a takeaway whenever the mood takes you!

How to Cook Your Favourite Takeaways at Home really is the answer to your prayers: the food you like to eat, when you want to eat it, at far less cost and with far more goodness!

Your Kitchen

There is no great secret to cooking delicious takeaways in your own kitchen. Just like any other style of cooking, you just need the know-how – and this book will show you how. There's no special equipment or unusual ingredients needed, but this chapter will highlight what you do need, and some basic rules for good practice in the kitchen.

Useful Equipment

No one has every piece of equipment they would like but here's a list of utensils and gadgets used in this book and what they're used for.

Baking sheets
Baking tins, various sizes
Casserole dishes, various, and at least one that's flameproof so you
    can use it directly on the hob as well as in the oven
Chopping boards, various
Colander or large sieve for straining cooked vegetables etc.
Fish slice for lifting foods out of a frying pan or from a baking sheet
Food processor and/or blender
Frying pans, large, medium and small
Grater
Kitchen scissors
Mixing bowls, various sizes
Ovenproof dishes, various sizes
Pie dishes, various sizes
Potato masher
Potato peeler
Roasting tins, various sizes
Saucepans, heavy-based, ideally non-stick, various sizes with lids
Sharp knives, at least one small one for vegetables etc., a bread knife

with a serrated edge, and a large chef's
knife
Slotted spoon, long-handled
Whisk, a balloon or wire one is ideal for
making sauces etc., plus an electric
hand whisk
Wooden kebab skewers
Wooden spoons

A Well-stocked Storecupboard

It's worth remembering that many of the
items you need for these recipes will keep
for months, stored correctly, so, after the
initial outlay, the dishes will become even
cheaper to make!

Here I've listed nearly everything I've used
(except for fresh produce). Obviously you're
not going to rush out and buy everything at
once but just build up your storecupboard
gradually as you need each ingredient.

- Always keep dried herbs and spices in
  small quantities in a dark, cool cupboard.
  That way they'll keep their colour and
  fragrance for several months.
- Store opened jars and bottles of purées
  and sauces in the fridge to keep them
  fresh as long as possible.
- Keep fresh vegetables in the chiller box
  in the fridge (except roots and tubers,
  which are best in a rack in a cool, dark
  cupboard).

Bottles, Jars and Tubes
Brown sauce
Chilli sauce, sweet
Dill pickled cucumbers, sliced
Honey, clear

Lemon juice
Lime juice
Mango chutney
Mayonnaise
Mirin (or dry sherry)
Miso paste: red and/or white
Oil: olive, sesame and sunflower
Olives: stoned black and green whole
and/or sliced
Passata
Pickled capers
Redcurrant jelly
Soy sauce: dark and/or light
Tamari (Japanese soy sauce)
Tomato ketchup
Tomato purée
Vinegar: white/red wine, malt, rice
Wasabi paste
Worcestershire sauce

Cans
Anchovies
Baked beans
Bamboo shoots
Beansprouts
Chickpeas
Coconut milk
Crabmeat
Garden peas
Haricot beans
Red kidney beans
Sweetcorn, kernels and creamed
Tomatoes, chopped
Water chestnuts

Dry Goods
Breadcrumbs, natural dried

Chapattis
Cornflour
Flour tortillas
Flour: plain and self-raising
Matzo meal
Naans
Noodles: Chinese medium egg, rice, udon
  and/or ramen
Nori wraps (dried seaweed sheets for
  sushi)
Pizza base mix
Popadoms, dried
Rice: basmati and sushi
Shiitake mushrooms, dried
Sugar: soft light brown and caster
Wakame (dried seaweed)

Dried Herbs, Spices, Nuts and Seeds

Basil
Bay leaves (or fresh if you have them in
  your garden)
Black mustard seeds
Cardamom pods
Celery salt or seeds
Chilli powder and dried flakes
Chilli purée (or use fresh)
Chinese five-spice powder
Cinnamon, ground
Cloves: whole and ground
Coriander, ground
Cumin, ground
Dill
Garam masala
Garlic cloves or purée
Ginger, fresh root or in a jar
Lemon grass purée
Madras curry powder

Mint
Mixed herbs
Mustard: American (mild), Dijon (or other
  French), English
Nigella or black onion seeds
Nutmeg, preferably whole to grate but
  otherwise ground
Onion and/or garlic granules
Oregano
Paprika: smoked and sweet
Peppercorns
Pickled ginger, vacuum-packed pink
Rosemary
Sage
Salt: fine and coarse sea
Sesame seeds
Turmeric, ground

Fridge

Bread (keeps better in the fridge)
Butter (preferably reduced fat)
Cheese: Cheddar (ready-grated is handy,
  low-fat is good), feta, mozzarella,
  paneer, Parmesan
Cream: single and double (or low-fat
  alternative)
Crème fraîche (half-fat is good)
Eggs
Milk, semi-skimmed
Plain low-fat yoghurt

Frozen Foods

Beef, minced
Chicken breasts
Chips (low-fat oven French fries, plain)
Coriander, chopped (or use fresh)
Lamb: minced and neck fillets

Onion, chopped
Parsley, chopped (or use fresh)
Pastry: filo, puff and shortcrust
Peas
Pork fillet
Prawns, cooked and peeled cold water
Root vegetables, mixed
Shallot, chopped
Spinach
Stir-fry vegetables

Everyday Fresh Vegetables
Carrots
Chillies
Cucumber
Herbs: basil, bay, coriander, parsley,
    rosemary
Lettuce
Onions: red and brown
Shallots
Peppers
Potatoes
Spring onions
Tomatoes

Basic Food Hygiene
A hygienic cook is a healthy cook, so – for your benefit and that of your diners – please bear the following in mind when you are preparing food.
- Always wash your hands before preparing food.
- Always wash and dry fresh produce before use.
- Don't lick your fingers.
- Don't keep tasting and stirring with the same spoon. Use a clean spoon every time you taste the food.
- Don't put raw and cooked meat on the same shelf in the fridge. Store raw meat on the bottom shelf, so it can't drip over other foods. Keep all perishable foods wrapped separately. Don't overfill the fridge or it will remain too warm. Remember, the coldest part of the fridge is at the bottom.
- Never use a cloth to wipe down a chopping board you have been using for cutting up meat, for instance, then use the same one to wipe down your work surfaces – you will simply spread germs. Always wash your cloth well in hot, soapy water.
- Preferably use separate boards for preparing meat, poultry, fish, vegetables and fruit, bread.
- Always transfer leftovers to a clean container and cover with a lid, clingfilm or foil. Cool as quickly as possible, then store in the fridge. Never put any warm food in the fridge.
- When reheating food, always make sure it is piping hot throughout, never just lukewarm. To test made-up dishes, such as lasagne or a pie, insert a knife down through the centre. Leave for 5 seconds, then remove. The blade should feel extremely hot. If not, heat the dish for a little longer.

Notes and conversion charts

CHAPTER 2

Notes on the Recipes

- The ingredients are listed in the order in which they are used in the recipe.
- All spoon measures are level unless otherwise stated.
- Eggs and vegetables are medium unless otherwise stated.
- Always wash, peel, core and deseed, if necessary, fresh produce before use. But deseeding fresh chillies is a matter of choice (some say it reduces the heat to remove the seeds).
- Seasoning is very much a matter of personal taste. Taste the food as you cook and adjust to suite your own palate.
- Fresh herbs are great for adding flavour and colour. Pots of basil and parsley for your windowsill are particularly good. The others are best bought in bunches and kept in the chiller box in the fridge.
- All can and packet sizes are approximate as they vary from brand to brand.
- Cooking times are approximate and should be used as a guide only. Always check food is piping hot and cooked through before serving.
- Always preheat the oven and cook on the shelf just above the centre unless otherwise stated (this isn't necessary in a fan oven where the temperature is similar throughout the oven).

Notes on Freezing

It's worth looking out for foods that are on special offer or reduced for quick sale to store in your freezer, as well as keeping it stocked up with basic essentials like bread (did you know you can take out slices from a loaf and toast straight from frozen?) and milk (always thaw completely then shake well as it separates when frozen). But when freezing there are some principles that must be followed.

- Only freeze top-quality produce. If it's overripe, damaged, or already past its best, it will deteriorate quickly as soon as it is defrosted.
- Foods that have been cooked and blanched foods should be covered and cooled quickly to room temperature, then frozen as soon as possible.
- Prepare and freeze raw foods separately from cooked.
- Pack in suitable freezer containers or bags, removing excess air to prevent oxidation. If you are using a container, press on the lid, then lift up one corner to release the air and re-seal. For bags, gently squeeze from the base up so the bag fits snugly over the food with no air pockets, then tie tight.
- Always label the food with contents, serving size and date (you think you'll remember but, trust me, you won't!).
- Don't freeze foods that specifically say they are not suitable for freezing. Some foods may already have been frozen, such as some fish, and others will simply spoil if frozen (cream and cheeses with less than 40 per cent fat content; caviar; egg-based custard, sauces and mayonnaise; eggs in their shells or hard-boiled; jam (except specific freezer jams); jelly made with gelatine; mayonnaise; salad stuffs; and plain low-fat yoghurt.
- Go by recommended freezer times. Food in the freezer doesn't last for ever. Depending on its composition, it will start to deteriorate after a while. It won't harm you but will definitely taste unpleasant and the texture may be impaired if you leave it in there too long.
- In general, freeze foods only once. Once thawed, raw food should be cooked and then can be refrozen. The few exceptions are:
  - Bread, which can safely be returned to the freezer once you've removed what you need to use;
  - Pastry, which you should keep as cool as possible but once rolled and made into a pie, for instance, can be frozen again before cooking (or unused filo sheets can safely be put back once you've removed the number you need to use);
  - Food that has been put straight from freezer to fridge and still has ice crystals in it will not have warmed enough to breed bacteria.
- Never re-freeze:
  - Thawed, cooked meats or poultry, pâtés, ready-cooked meat or poultry dishes;
  - Uncooked dishes made with thawed, frozen cooked meats or fish – like mousses or sandwiches;
  - Dishes made with cooked leftover meat, like a cottage pie made with minced beef from the Sunday joint;
  - Foods that have thawed completely at room temperature;
  - Melted ice cream.

Conversion Charts

Those who prefer Imperial measures can use these conversions (they are approximate for ease of use).

For convenience, I sometimes use cup measures as it's so easy for things like rice or couscous. You can use American cup measuring sets, just an ordinary cup or a measuring jug. A cup is 250ml, or whatever volume fits into the space (so a cup of sugar is 225g whereas a cup of flour is 100g).

OVEN TEMPERATURES										
110°C	120°C	140°C	150°C	160°C	180°C	190°C	200°C	220°C	230°C	240°C
225°F	250°F	275°F	300°F	325°F	350°F	375°F	400°F	425°F	450°F	475°F
gas ¼	gas ½	gas 1	gas 2	gas 3	gas 4	gas 5	gas 6	gas 7	gas 8	gas 9

WEIGHT										
25g	50g	75g	100g	150g	175g	200g	225g	250g	300g	450g
1oz	2oz	3oz	4oz	5oz	6oz	7oz	8oz	9oz	10oz	1lb

MEASUREMENTS										
1cm	5cm	10cm	13cm	15cm	18cm	20cm	25cm	30cm	35cm	40cm
½ in	2 in	4 in	5 in	6 in	7 in	8 in	10 in	12 in	14 in	16 in

LIQUID MEASURE										
5ml	15ml	50ml	75ml	100ml	125ml	150ml	200ml	300ml	450ml	600ml
1 tsp	1 tbls	2 fl oz	3 fl oz	4 fl oz	4½ fl oz	5 fl oz	7 fl oz	½ pt	¾ pt	1 pt

From the Curry House

Everyone loves an Indian takeaway but you don't have to limit yourself to the Friday night curry any more. You can enjoy great-tasting Indian-style dishes any time.

Some curries are at their best if you allow them to cook slowly, so you are best to cook these in advance. But the good news is that they taste even better when reheated thoroughly. The other option is to use a pressure cooker – to speed things up – or a slow cooker – to put you in control, and I have included tips for both so you can use whatever suits you best.

You'll also find all your favourite side dishes and accompaniments, so you can create complete – and completely delicious – Indian-style meals.

For specific curries – like Vindaloo, Rogan Josh or Tandoori – you could use a ready-mixed spice paste from a jar instead of the individual spices, if you prefer; I've indicated in the speed tip how much to use. But it's great fun to use the authentic individual spices, and as many of the recipes use similar spices in different quantities and ratios, you'll not need to buy too many spices, which will be a lot cheaper than buying ready-made pastes.

Takeaway Tip

Fat-free popadoms: Ready-cooked popadoms have been fried and are quite greasy. For a healthier (and cheaper) option, buy a pack of dried popadoms (plain or with various spices). They'll keep for months in the cupboard. Pop them one at a time in the microwave and cook on High for up to 30 seconds each side until puffy all over. Alternatively cook them under the grill (but they have a habit of burning the minute your back is turned!).

Preparation time:
10 minutes plus marinating
Cooking time:
40 minutes
To freeze: Only freeze if you
have used fresh chicken (not
thawed, frozen); freeze
uncooked in the marinade in a
sealable freezer bag for up to
1 month; thaw overnight in the
fridge, then cook as above

4 chicken leg portions, cut in
   2 at the leg joint (or
   4 chicken thighs and
   4 drumsticks), skin
   removed
150ml thick, plain yoghurt
2 garlic cloves, crushed (or
   1 tsp garlic purée)
1 tbsp lemon juice
2 tsp garam masala
1 tbsp sweet paprika
1 tsp grated fresh root ginger
   (or ginger purée)
Salt and freshly ground black
   pepper

To garnish
Shredded lettuce, tomato
   wedges, diced cucumber
   and lemon wedges

To serve
Baked Vegetable Pilau (page
   42) and mango chutney

Serves 4

Tandoori Chicken

This dish is traditionally cooked a clay oven and we can't replicate that, but this version tastes great and makes full use of your oven as it is served with Baked Pilau Rice, saving fuel and effort. Try serving it with the Mixed Vegetable Curry (page 37) too.

Speed tip: Use 1–2 tbsp tandoori paste or powder instead of all the flavourings

- Make several slashes in the flesh of the chicken with a sharp knife.

- Mix the remaining ingredients together in a large, shallow dish.

- Add the chicken and rub the mixture well into the slits. Cover the dish with clingfilm and marinate in the fridge for a couple of hours or up to 24 hours as convenient.

- Preheat the oven to 220°C/gas 7.

- Drain the chicken and place in a roasting tin. Bake in the oven for about 40 minutes until well browned in places and the juices run clear when pierced with a skewer in the thickest part.

- Meanwhile make the rice on page 42 and place in the oven with the chicken whilst it's cooking, and prepare the garnish.

- When the chicken is cooked, remove it from the oven and leave to rest with the rice.

- Place the chicken on plates with the rice and garnish with the salad and lemon wedges. Serve with mango chutney.

• From the Curry House

Serves 4

Chicken Tikka Masala

Preparation time:
10 minutes plus marinating
Cooking time:
20 minutes
To freeze:
Cool quickly, then freeze in rigid containers for up to 3 months

This is the most popular Indian takeaway so had to be included. The chicken is usually marinated in yoghurt and spices then grilled before adding to the sauce at the last moment. But here it's just quickly fried off, which saves time and washing up!

Speed tip: Use 3 tbsp Tikka Masala paste instead of the spices and lime juice

- Mix the garlic, ginger, chilli and spices with the lime juice, yoghurt and 2 tbsp of the oil. Add the chicken and toss well to coat in the mixture. Cover with clingfilm and leave to marinate in the fridge for a couple of hours or up to 24 hours.

- Heat the remaining oil in a large saucepan. Add the onions and peppers and fry, stirring, for about 3 minutes until soft and slightly golden.

- Add the chicken and all the spice mixture and fry quickly, stirring, for 2–3 minutes to brown.

- Add the tomatoes, tomato purée, stock and bay leaf. Bring to the boil, then reduce the heat and simmer gently for 15 minutes until the chicken and vegetables are tender, stirring occasionally.

- Stir in the mango chutney and crème fraîche, seasoning to taste with salt and pepper. Reheat but do not boil.

2 garlic cloves, crushed (or 1 tsp garlic purée)
2 tsp grated fresh root ginger (or ginger purée)
1 fresh green or red chilli, finely chopped (or $\frac{1}{4}$–$\frac{1}{2}$ tsp chilli purée)
$\frac{1}{2}$ tsp chilli powder
1 tsp ground cumin
1 tsp garam masala
$\frac{1}{2}$ tsp ground turmeric
1 tbsp sweet paprika
1 tbsp lime juice
2 tbsp plain yoghurt
4 tbsp sunflower oil
500g diced boneless chicken
2 onions, halved and thinly sliced (or 2 large handfuls of frozen chopped onion)
2 red peppers, diced
400g can of chopped tomatoes
1 tbsp tomato purée
200ml chicken stock
1 bay leaf
1 tbsp smooth mango chutney
200ml crème fraîche
Salt and freshly ground black pepper

To serve
Sag Aloo (page 35) or Quick Naan Bread (page 43) or bought nan bread.

Preparation time:
10 minutes
Cooking time:
20 minutes
To freeze:
Cool quickly, freeze in rigid
containers for up to 3 months

Serves 4

Quick Chicken Madras

1 tbsp lemon or lime juice
1 garlic clove, crushed (or
   ½ tsp garlic purée)
2 tsp garam masala
½ tsp salt
500g diced boneless chicken
   (or 4 small skinless
   breasts, diced)
2 tbsp sunflower oil
1 large onion, chopped (or
   2 large handfuls of frozen
   chopped onion)
2 tbsp Madras curry powder
400g can of chopped
   tomatoes
60g creamed coconut, cut
   into pieces
300ml water
1 tbsp tomato purée
1 tbsp mango chutney
2 tbsp chopped fresh or
   frozen coriander

To serve
Extra mango chutney, Quick
   Naan Bread (page 43 or
   use bought) and a large
   mixed salad

This uses Madras curry powder (great for your storecupboard as it has a good flavour for any quick, curry-flavoured dish). Vary the amount to reduce or increase the heat. Instead of salad, cook some green beans and throw them in at the last minute.

- Mix together the lemon or lime juice, garlic, garam masala and salt. Add the chicken and turn over in the mixture to coat completely.

- Heat the oil in a large saucepan. Add the onion and fry, stirring, for 3–4 minutes until lightly golden.

- Stir in the curry powder and cook, stirring, for 30 seconds.

- Add the chicken and fry, stirring, until lightly browned all over.

- Add the tomatoes, coconut, water, tomato purée and mango chutney. Bring to the boil, then reduce the heat and simmer gently for 15 minutes, stirring occasionally, until the sauce is rich and thick and the chicken is tender.

- Stir in the coriander. Taste and re-season if necessary.

- Serve with mango chutney, naan bread and a mixed salad.

● From the Curry House

Serves 4

Chicken Tikka

Preparation time:
5 minutes plus marinating
Cooking time:
15 minutes
To freeze:
Best eaten fresh

Tikka means 'bits' and this recipe is simply marinated chicken 'bits' grilled on skewers. Make sure you have the grill good and hot before you start, or use a griddle pan so that you can get nice charred bits as you cook them.

- Mix everything except the chicken in a large plastic container with a lid. Add the chicken, mix well, cover and leave in the fridge for at least 2 hours or all day or overnight, if more convenient.

- Preheat the grill.

- Drain the chicken of excess marinade. Thread on 8 soaked wooden skewers. Grill, turning once or twice, for about 15 minutes or until cooked through and slightly charred at the edges. Serve hot.

90ml thick plain yoghurt
2 large garlic cloves (or 2 tsp garlic purée)
2 tsp grated fresh root ginger (or ginger purée)
½ tsp chilli powder
1 tbsp lemon or lime juice
1 tbsp sweet paprika
1 tbsp garam masala
1 tsp soft light brown sugar
¼ tsp salt
Freshly ground black pepper
2 tbsp finely chopped fresh or frozen coriander
500g diced skinless chicken breast (or 4 small breasts, cut in bite-sized chunks)

To serve
Lime or lemon wedges, dhal (pages 38–39) and Quick Naan (page 43) or ready-made naan bread

Preparation time:
5 minutes
Cooking time:
17 minutes
To freeze:
Not suitable for freezing

Serves 4

Quick Prawn Curry

2 tbsp sunflower oil
1 large onion, chopped (or 2
    large handfuls of frozen
    chopped onion)
3 tbsp Madras curry powder
1 tbsp lemon or lime juice
1 garlic clove, crushed
    (or ½ tsp garlic purée)
2 tsp garam masala
½ tsp salt
400g can of chopped
    tomatoes
1 tbsp tomato purée
4 tbsp desiccated coconut
2 tsp soft light brown sugar
120ml water
400g cooked, peeled
    prawns, thawed if frozen
2 tbsp chopped fresh or
    frozen coriander
Salt and freshly ground black
    pepper

To serve
Plain basmati rice and a
    large mixed salad

This is great to throw together quickly when you get home. Just make the sauce then throw in the prawns for the last 2–3 minutes. Put the pan of water for the rice on before you start cooking or you'll have to wait for it – the recipe's that quick!

- Heat the oil in a large saucepan. Add the onion and fry, stirring, for 3–4 minutes until lightly golden.

- Stir in the curry powder and cook, stirring, for 30 seconds.

- Add the remaining ingredients except the prawns and half the coriander. Bring to the boil, reduce the heat and simmer very gently for 5–10 minutes until thick.

- Stir in the prawns and the remaining coriander and simmer, stirring gently, for 2–3 minutes until the prawns are heated through. Taste and re-season if necessary.

- Serve on a bed of rice with a mixed salad.

• From the Curry House

Serves 4

Pork Vindaloo

Preparation time:
10 minutes plus marinating
Cooking time:
50 minutes
To freeze:
Cool quickly, place in rigid
containers with a sealable lids
and freeze for up to 3 months

This is a hot, sharp curry from Goa in Southern India. It can be cooked immediately but the flavour is better if the meat is left to marinate all day or overnight. You can use diced lamb neck fillets or chicken instead of pork. Reduce the chilli if you can't stand the heat!

Speed tip: Use 2 tbsp Vindaloo paste instead of the onion, spices and half the vinegar

- In a large plastic container with a lid, mix the grated onion with the spices, ginger, garlic and enough of the vinegar to make a paste. Add the pork and toss well with your hands so it is all well coated in the paste. Ideally, cover and leave to marinate for several hours (or overnight if that suits you better).

- Heat the oil in a large heavy-based pan. Add the pork and marinade and fry, stirring, for 2–3 minutes.

- Add the tomatoes, the remaining vinegar, the water and a little salt. Bring to the boil, then reduce the heat and simmer gently for about 45 minutes, stirring occasionally, until the sauce is rich and thick, and the pork is tender.

- Garnish with fresh coriander, if using, and serve with plain rice, cucumber raita, a large mixed salad and mango chutney.

1 onion, grated
1 tsp English mustard
2 tsp chilli powder
1 tsp ground cinnamon
1½ tsp ground cumin
½ tsp ground cloves
½ tsp ground turmeric
2 tsp grated fresh root
  ginger (or ginger purée)
2 garlic cloves, crushed (or
  1 tsp garlic purée)
90ml white wine vinegar
700g pork fillet or leg, diced
2 tbsp sunflower oil
400g can of chopped
  tomatoes
200ml water
Salt

To garnish
Chopped fresh coriander
  (optional)

To serve
Plain rice, Cucumber Raita
  (page 34), a large mixed
  salad and mango chutney

Preparation time:
10 minutes
Cooking time:
20 minutes
To freeze:
Cool quickly, pack in rigid
containers and freeze for up to
2 months

2 tbsp sunflower oil
1 large onion, chopped (or a
    large handful of frozen
    chopped onion)
2 garlic cloves, crushed (or
    1 tsp garlic purée)
500g lean minced beef
1–2 tbsp Madras curry
    powder
2 tsp grated fresh root
    ginger (or ginger purée)
300ml beef stock
1 tbsp tomato purée
175g frozen peas
Salt

To serve
Plain basmati rice and a
    large tomato and onion
    salad topped with lots of
    fresh, chopped coriander,
    mint or parsley

Serves 4

Keema Curry with Peas

This is another very quick meal. You could use minced lamb instead of beef and increase the heat by adding an extra tablespoon of curry powder. Ring the changes with frozen baby carrots or cut green beans but it's best to thaw them first so they cook in time.

* Heat the oil in a large saucepan. Add the onion and garlic and fry gently, stirring, for 3 minutes until softened but not browned.

* Add the minced beef and fry, stirring, until it is no longer pink and all the grains are separate.

* Stir in the curry powder and fry for a further 1 minute, stirring.

* Add the ginger, stock and tomato purée. Bring to the boil, stirring, then reduce the heat and simmer gently for 15 minutes, stirring from time to time. (Meanwhile, cook the rice.)

* Add the peas and simmer for a further 5 minutes. Season to taste with salt.

* Serve spooned over basmati rice with mango chutney and a tomato salad with lots of fresh chopped coriander, mint or parsley thrown over.

• From the Curry House

Serves 4

Palak Gosht

Preparation time:
10 minutes
Cooking time:
15 minutes
To freeze:
It's as quick to cook fresh as
thaw and reheat but, if you
wish, cool quickly and freeze in
rigid containers for up to 3
months

A quick lamb curry for when time is short, this uses lamb neck fillets – look for frozen ones as they're much cheaper than fresh. Simply thaw them in the fridge overnight before use. Try it with diced chicken breasts, too.

- Heat the oil in a saucepan. Add the onion and garlic and fry, stirring, for 2 minutes until softened but not browned.

- Add the lamb, all the spices and the mushrooms and cook, stirring, until the meat is browned on all sides.

- Add the stock, raisins and sugar, part-cover the pan and simmer for 10 minutes.

- Add the spinach to the lamb and sprinkle with a little salt. Cook for about 3 minutes, stirring occasionally, until the spinach has wilted and the sauce has reduced and thickened slightly. Taste and re-season if necessary.

- Serve with plain basmati rice and carrot salad.

1 tbsp sunflower oil
1 onion, chopped (or a large
    handful of frozen chopped
    onion)
1 garlic clove, crushed (or
    $\frac{1}{2}$ tsp garlic purée)
450g lamb neck fillet, cut
    into bite-sized pieces
1 tsp grated fresh root
    ginger (or ginger purée)
1 tbsp Madras curry powder
2 tsp sweet paprika
$\frac{1}{2}$ tsp ground cinnamon
100g cup mushrooms,
    quartered
200ml lamb or chicken stock
Handful of raisins
1 tsp caster sugar
200g spinach, well washed
    and drained
Salt

To serve
    Plain basmati rice and
    Indian Carrot Salad (page
    40)

Preparation time:
15 minutes

Cooking time:
80 minutes

To freeze:
Cool quickly, then freeze in portions in sealable bags for up to 3 months

Serves 4

Lamb Biryani

2 tbsp sunflower oil
2 large onions, sliced
500g diced lean lamb
1 tsp grated fresh root
  ginger (or ginger purée)
1 garlic clove, crushed (or
  ½ tsp garlic purée)
¼ tsp chilli powder
1 tsp ground cumin
1 tsp ground coriander
1 tsp ground turmeric
1 bay leaf
Salt and freshly ground black
  pepper
250ml plain yoghurt
250ml lamb or chicken stock
350g basmati rice
100g frozen peas

To garnish
2 tbsp raisins or currants
2 tbsp toasted flaked
  coconut or almonds

To serve
Popadoms, Cucumber Raita
  (page 34) and a mixed
  salad

You can use leftover roast lamb or chicken. Simply dice it and add to the onions, omit the stock and just add the spices and yoghurt, then simmer for 20 minutes until the sauce is thick. Add the cooked rice and continue as in the recipe. If you have less meat, add more peas.

Speed tip: Use 1–2 tbsp Biryani paste instead of the ginger, chilli, cumin, coriander and turmeric

- Heat the oil in a large saucepan. Add the onions and fry for about 5 minutes, stirring until soft and golden. Remove half and reserve for garnish. Add the lamb to the remaining onion and brown on all sides. Add all the spices, the bay leaf and a little salt and pepper. Cook, stirring, for 1 minute.

- Stir in the yoghurt and the stock. Bring to the boil, then reduce the heat, cover and simmer gently for 1 hour.

- Remove the lid and continue to simmer, stirring occasionally, for a further 5–10 minutes until the liquid has evaporated and the meat is tender and bathed in a rich sauce.

- Meanwhile, cook the rice in boiling, salted water for 10 minutes, adding the peas half way through cooking. Drain and return to the pan. Add the lamb to the rice, stirring well. Taste and re-season, if necessary.

- Meanwhile, reheat the extra fried onions and stir in the dried fruit and nuts.

- Spoon the biryani on to plates, garnish with the fruit and nut mixture, and serve with popadoms, a side salad and cucumber raita.

• From the Curry House

Serves 4

Lamb Rogan Josh

Preparation time:
10 minutes
Cooking time:
45 minutes
To freeze:
Cool quickly, then pack in rigid
containers and freeze for up to
3 months

This mild curry is good made with diced beef (but simmer it for 1½ hours) or chicken (simmer for 20 minutes). I've added carrots and cabbage as they go particularly well but you could use cauliflower florets and diced butternut squash instead.

Speed tip: Use 2–3 tbsp Rogan Josh curry paste instead of all the spices, and omit the fennel seeds. Use 4 handfuls of frozen stew vegetables instead of preparing your own

- Heat the oil in a saucepan and fry the fennel seeds, if using, for 30 seconds until fragrant.

- Add the lamb and brown on all sides.

- Add all the spices and the ginger and garlic and fry, stirring, for about 1 minute.

- Add the vegetables, yoghurt, stock, sugar and tomato purée. Stir well. Bring to the boil (it will curdle), then reduce the heat, cover and simmer gently for about 45 minutes or until the lamb is really tender and bathed in a rich sauce.

- Taste and re-season, if necessary.

- Serve with Bombay potatoes and mango chutney.

1 tbsp sunflower oil
1 tbsp fennel seeds
   (optional)
500g lean leg or neck fillet
   of lamb, diced (not too
   big)
½ tsp ground cinnamon
1 tbsp ground cumin
1 tbsp paprika
¼ tsp ground cloves
¼ tsp ground cardamom
1 tsp garam masala
¼ tsp chilli powder
1 tsp grated fresh root
   ginger (or ginger purée)
2 garlic cloves, crushed (or
   1 tsp garlic purée)
2 large carrots, sliced
½ small white cabbage, core
   removed and shredded
200ml plain yoghurt
200ml lamb or chicken stock
½ tsp caster sugar
2 tbsp tomato purée
Salt

To serve
Bombay Aloo (page 36),
   mango chutney and a
   mixed salad

To slow cook:
Reduce the quantities of yoghurt and stock to 150ml each. After bringing to the boil, tip into the crock pot and cook on LOW for 8–10 hours

To pressure cook:
Reduce the quantities of yoghurt and stock to 150ml each. Cook on HIGH for 15 minutes, reduce the pressure quickly under cold water, then boil rapidly in the open pan, if necessary, to thicken the sauce

Preparation time:
15 minutes plus marinating
Cooking time:
60–90 minutes
To freeze:
Cool quickly, then freeze in rigid
containers for up to 3 months

Serves 4

Lamb Korma

2 large garlic cloves, crushed
(or 1 tsp garlic purée)
1 tbsp grated fresh root
ginger (or ginger purée)
1 tsp ground turmeric
½ tsp ground cinnamon
Good pinch of chilli powder
500ml water
700g lean diced lamb
2 tbsp sunflower oil
25g butter or ghee
2 onions, finely chopped (or
2 large handfuls of
chopped frozen onion)
1 tsp caster sugar
Salt and freshly ground black
pepper
120ml single cream

To garnish
Lemon wedges

To serve
Baked Vegetable Pilau
Rice (page 42) and a
green salad

To slow cook:
Reduce the quantity of water to
250ml. After bringing to the
boil, tip into the crock pot and
cook on LOW for 8–10 hours

To pressure cook:
Reduce the quantity of liquid
to 250ml. Cook on HIGH for
15 minutes, then reduce the
pressure quickly. Boil rapidly in
open pan, if necessary, to
thicken sauce

This mild, creamy curry can be cooked on the hob for the same amount of time (and cook Simple Pilau Rice (page 41) instead of the baked pilau). You can use diced chicken instead of lamb, but halve the cooking time. Marinating improves the flavour but is not essential.

Speed tip: Use 1–2 tbsp Korma curry paste instead of the ginger, turmeric, cinnamon and chilli powder

• Mix the garlic and spices together with 4 tbsp of the water to form a paste in a large plastic container with a lid. Add the meat and mix well with your hands. Cover and leave to marinate in the fridge for several hours or overnight if more convenient.

• Preheat the oven to 180°C/gas 4.

• Heat the oil and butter or ghee in a large flameproof casserole. Add the onions and fry, stirring, for 3–4 minutes until golden. Add the meat and fry, stirring, until browned all over.

• Stir in the remaining water, the sugar and some salt and pepper. Bring to the boil, stir well, cover tightly (using foil as well as a lid, if necessary), and cook in the oven for 1½ hours or until the lamb is tender and bathed in sauce.

• Meanwhile prepare the rice and put in the oven to cook at the same time.

• Stir in the cream, taste and re-season if necessary.

• Garnish with lemon wedges and serve with baked vegetable pilau rice and a green salad.

• From the Curry House

Makes 8

Onion Bhajis

Preparation time:
10 minutes
Cooking time:
5 minutes
To freeze:
Cool quickly, place in a sealable freezer bag and freeze for up to 3 months; thaw before reheating briefly in a hot oven

If you really like these, make a larger batch and freeze them for future use. They can be thawed and reheated in the oven along with a thawed frozen curry. They're actually tasty cold for a quick and simple lunch, too, served with an Indian Carrot Salad (page 40).

50g gram (chickpea) flour (or use plain flour)
¼ tsp salt
¼ tsp ground turmeric
½ tsp garam masala
½ tsp ground cumin
3–4 tbsp tepid water
1 onion, chopped (or 2 handfuls of frozen chopped onion)
Sunflower oil for frying

- Mix the flour salt and spices together with enough water to form a thick cream. Stir in the onion.

- Heat about 1cm sunflower oil in a deep frying pan to 190°C or until a piece of the chopped onion dropped into it immediately rises to the surface of the oil, sizzling.

- Add rough spoonfuls of the mixture to the hot oil and fry for 4–5 minutes until golden, turning once.

- Drain thoroughly on kitchen paper and serve hot.

Preparation time:
40 minutes
Cooking time:
15–20 minutes
To freeze:
Cool quickly, pack in sealable freezer bags and freeze for up to 3 months; thaw before reheating briefly in a hot oven

1 large potato (about 225g)
1 tbsp sunflower oil, plus extra for brushing
1 small onion, chopped (or a handful of frozen chopped onion)
1 tsp ground cumin
$\frac{1}{4}$ tsp chilli powder
1 tsp ground turmeric
1 tsp garam masala
300g can of garden peas in water, drained, reserving the water
1 tbsp chopped fresh or frozen coriander
Salt and freshly ground black pepper
4 large sheets filo pastry

To serve
Mango chutney or Cucumber Raita (page 34)

Makes 32

Mini Vegetable Samosas

It's worth making a whole batch of these as they can be kept in the fridge for several days or frozen (see above left). They taste good served cold for a quick lunch with salad too. Use cooked leftover potato if you have it – you need about 175g.

Speed tip: Make 8 large samosas instead of all the very tiny ones. Cut the filo sheets in half, then fold each in half to form a big triangle. Divide the mixture between them and fold as below

- If you are using a hob, peel the potato, cut into small pieces and cook in boiling water until tender, then drain and mash. If you prefer a microwave, prick the potato all over and microwave for about 4 minutes until soft then, when cool enough to handle, peel and mash in a bowl.

- Heat 1 tbsp oil in a frying pan and fry the onion for 3 minutes, stirring until soft and lightly golden.

- Add the spices and fry for 30 seconds.

- Remove from the heat and tip into the potato. Add the peas and enough of the reserved liquid to moisten the mixture thoroughly so it is soft but not wet (you may need nearly all of it depending on the potato). Stir in the coriander and season with salt and pepper. Mix thoroughly and set aside to cool.

- Brush a sheet of filo with a little oil. Fold in half. Cut in quarters, then cut each quarter in half diagonally to make 8 small equal triangles. Divide the filling into quarters and, using one quarter, divide that mixture between the centres of the 8 triangles. Brush the edges with water.

● From the Curry House

- Preheat the oven to 200°C/gas 6 and lightly oil 2 or 3 baking sheets.

- For each triangle, take one side point and fold it up over to meet the centre point. Fold those two points down over the pastry to form a straight edge. Fold the open pastry over to meet the opposite point to form a filled triangle. Press the edges together to seal. (It sounds complicated but it isn't when you do it!).

- Repeat with the other three filo sheets and filling.

- Place on the baking sheets and brush with a little more oil.

- Bake in the oven for 15–20 minutes until crisp and golden.

- Serve hot or cold with mango chutney or raita.

Serves 4

Cucumber Raita

120ml thick plain yoghurt
5cm piece cucumber, grated
  or finely chopped
2 tbsp chopped fresh or
  2 tsp dried mint
Salt and freshly ground black
  pepper

This light, cooling condiment is ideal served with crunchy popadoms or onion bhajis as a starter or to accompany any curry. You can make simple mint raita by omitting the cucumber and flavouring the yoghurt with mint sauce from a jar to taste.

• Put the yoghurt in a small bowl.

• Squeeze the cucumber to remove any excess moisture, then stir into the yoghurt with the mint and salt and pepper to taste.

• Chill until ready to serve.

• From the Curry House

Serves 4

Sag Aloo

Preparation time:
10 minutes
Cooking time:
15–20 minutes
To freeze:
Not suitable for freezing

Spinach and potato curry is a delicious side dish to serve with any meat or chicken curry but it's also great for a light meal with extra tomatoes and either some cubes of paneer cheese added, or served topped with poached eggs, with some naan bread.

- Squeeze the spinach, if using frozen, to remove excess moisture. Set aside.

- Heat the oil in a large saucepan. Add the onion and garlic and fry, stirring, for 2 minutes.

- Add the remaining ingredients except the spinach and tomatoes. Bring to the boil, then reduce the heat, part-cover and simmer for 10 minutes.

- Add the spinach and tomatoes, stir gently, cover and cook for a further 5–10 minutes until the vegetables are tender but the tomatoes still have some shape. Taste and re-season if necessary.

400g well-washed fresh or
 thawed frozen spinach
2 tbsp sunflower oil
1 large onion, halved and
 thinly sliced (or 2 large
 handfuls of frozen
 chopped onion)
1 large garlic clove, crushed
 (or $\frac{1}{2}$ tsp garlic purée)
1 tsp ground cumin
$\frac{1}{2}$ tsp ground turmeric
2 large potatoes, peeled and
 cut into bite-sized chunks
1 green pepper, cut into
 chunks
Good pinch of chilli powder
200ml water
Salt
2 tomatoes, quartered

Preparation time:
10 minutes
Cooking time:
20 minutes
To freeze:
Best eaten fresh

Serves 4

Bombay Aloo

700g potatoes, peeled and
   cut into walnut-sized
   pieces
Salt
2 tbsp sunflower oil
2 green chillies, deseeded (if
   liked) and finely chopped
   (or ½–1 tsp chilli purée)
1 tsp ground cumin
1 tsp ground coriander
¼ tsp ground turmeric
400g can of chopped
   tomatoes
Good pinch of caster sugar
2 tbsp chopped fresh or
   frozen coriander

Bombay potatoes is a particular favourite as a snack (try the pieces speared on cocktail sticks with a cucumber raita or some mango chutney to dip into) or as an accompaniment to any curry for a change from rice.

- Boil the potatoes in lightly salted water for about 10 minutes until just tender but still holding their shape. Drain.

- Meanwhile, heat the oil in a large non-stick pan and fry the spices over a moderate heat, stirring, for 30 seconds.

- Add the tomatoes and sugar, stir, then fry for 2–3 minutes.

- Add the potatoes and stir and turn gently until they are coated in the spicy tomatoes. Sprinkle with just a little salt. Cover with a lid, reduce the heat and cook for about 10 minutes, stirring occasionally so the potatoes don't stick to the pan.

- Add the coriander and stir and turn one more time. Serve hot.

• From the Curry House

Serves 4

Mixed Vegetable Curry

Preparation time:
15 minutes
Cooking time:
25 minutes
To freeze:
Cool quickly, pack into a rigid
container and freeze for up to 6
months; note that if you use a
lot of potato, they pieces may
be a little watery when thawed

The great thing about a vegetable curry is you can add any veggies you have to hand, from roots like turnips and swede to courgettes, green beans or anything that takes your fancy. Experiment with what looks lovely and fresh at the supermarket and enjoy!

Speed tip: Use 1 tbsp Madras curry powder instead of the cumin, turmeric, chilli powder and garam masala

- Heat the oil in a large saucepan. Add the onion and garlic and fry, stirring, for 2 minutes.

- Add the spices and fry for 30 seconds.

- Stir in the coconut, water and tomato purée. Bring to the boil, stirring until the coconut has melted.

- Stir in the lime juice and salt.

- Add all the vegetables and stir gently. Tuck in the bay leaf. Bring back to the boil, reduce the heat, cover and simmer very gently for about 20 minutes, stirring occasionally, or until all the vegetables are tender and bathed in a rich sauce.

- Taste and re-season if necessary. Discard the bay leaf before serving.

2 tbsp sunflower oil
1 large garlic clove, crushed
  (or ½ tsp garlic purée)
1 large onion, chopped (or a
  large handful of frozen
  chopped onion)
2 tsp ground cumin
1 tsp ground turmeric
¼ tsp chilli powder
  (optional)
1 tbsp garam masala
150g creamed coconut, cut
  into small pieces
600ml water
2 tbsp tomato purée
1 tbsp lime juice
1 tsp salt
1 large carrot, sliced
1 small aubergine, cut into
  small chunks
1 small green pepper, sliced
1 large potato, peeled and
  cut into chunks
½ small cauliflower, cut into
  florets
Large handful of fresh or
  frozen green beans, cut
  into short lengths
1 bay leaf

Preparation time:
5 minutes

Cooking time:
5 minutes

To freeze:
Best eaten fresh

Serves 4

Instant Dal

410g can of pease pudding
6 tbsp water
1 tbsp smooth mango
  chutney
3 tbsp sunflower oil
1 onion, chopped (or a large
  handful of frozen chopped
  onion)
1 tbsp Madras curry powder
Salt

This is so quick, it's virtually instant! And it is the perfect accompaniment to any of the Indian curries in this book. It's also nice spread on naan breads for a quick snack with some sliced cucumber or shredded lettuce, or thinned with stock as a soup.

- Empty the contents of the can of pease pudding into a non-stick pan and add the water. Stir over a low heat, breaking up the pease pudding and stirring until piping hot. Stir in the mango chutney.

- Meanwhile, heat the oil in a frying pan and fry the onion, stirring, for 3–4 minutes until golden and soft. Add the Madras curry powder and fry for 30 seconds, stirring continuously.

- Add the onions to the pease pudding and stir together well. Season to taste with salt. Serve hot.

• From the Curry House

Serves 4

Masoor Dal

Preparation time:
5 minutes
Cooking time:
25–30 minutes
To freeze:
Cool quickly, then pack in rigid containers, seal and freeze for up to 6 months

Red lentils don't need pre-soaking and are packed with goodness. They're perfect to serve with dryer dishes or as a great light meal on their own. Try stirring in cubes of paneer or Cheddar cheese before serving with naan bread and a green salad for supper.

> **Speed tip:** Add 1 tbsp Madras curry powder to the onions instead of the cumin, coriander, paprika and chilli powder

- Put the lentils in a large saucepan with the garlic, turmeric and ginger. Add the stock or water. Stir well, bring to the boil, then reduce the heat, cover and simmer for 25–30 minutes until pulpy and the water has been absorbed, stirring occasionally.

- Meanwhile, heat the oil and butter or ghee in a small pan. Add the onion and fry for about 5 minutes, stirring until golden and cooked through.

- Stir in the remaining ingredients except the salt and fry for 30 seconds. Remove from the heat.

- When the lentils are cooked, stir in the onion mixture, season to taste with salt and serve hot.

175g red lentils
1 garlic clove, crushed (or ½ tsp garlic purée)
1 tsp ground turmeric
1 tsp grated fresh root ginger (or ginger purée)
500ml chicken or vegetable stock, or water
2 tbsp sunflower oil
30g butter or ghee
1 onion, sliced (or a large handful of frozen chopped onion)
1 tsp ground cumin
1 tsp ground coriander
2 tsp paprika
¼ tsp chilli powder
Salt

Preparation time:
8 minutes

Cooking time:
30 seconds

To freeze:
Best eaten fresh

Serves 4

Indian Carrot Salad

4 large carrots
1 tbsp lemon juice
Salt and freshly ground black
   pepper
2 tbsp sunflower oil
1 tbsp cumin seeds

If you have a food processor, use it to grate the carrots – it's so much easier than using a hand grater! Use coarsly crushed coriander seeds for a change. Try mixing half beetroot and half carrots too for a delicious added dimension.

- Peel and grate the carrots into a salad bowl. Add the lemon juice and a sprinkling of salt and freshly ground black pepper. Toss the ingredients together gently.

- Heat the oil in a frying pan. Add the cumin seeds and fry for about 30 seconds until fragrant.

- Pour over the carrots, toss and serve.

• From the Curry House

Serves 4

Simple Pilau Rice

Preparation time:
5 minutes
Cooking time:
20 minutes plus standing time
To freeze:
Cool quickly, freeze in sealable
freezer bags for up to 6 months

For Yellow Rice, simply add 1 tsp ground turmeric to the mixture. For Vegetable Rice, throw in some finely diced carrots, courgettes, cut green beans or perhaps some colourful diced peppers and some frozen peas with the rice.

- Soak the rice in the water for about 30 minutes.

- Heat the oil in a heavy-based saucepan and fry the spices for 30 seconds, stirring.

- Add the rice and soaking water. Crumble in the stock cube or add the concentrate and add a pinch of salt and a good grinding of pepper. Bring to the boil, then reduce the heat as low as possible, cover tightly with foil then the lid and cook for 20 minutes.

- Remove from the heat and leave to stand for 5 minutes then remove the lid and fluff up with a fork before serving.

225g basmati rice
550ml water
2 tbsp sunflower oil
2 cardamom pods, split
1 piece of cinnamon stick
4 cloves
1 chicken or vegetable stock
  cube or 1 tbsp stock
  concentrate
Salt and freshly ground black
  pepper

Preparation time:
10 minutes

Cooking time:
20 or 30 minutes plus standing time

To freeze:
Cool quickly, freeze in sealable freezer bags for up to 6 months

Serves 4

Baked Vegetable Pilau Rice

2 tbsp sunflower oil
1 onion, finely chopped (or a large handful of frozen chopped onion)
2 carrots, finely diced
1 red pepper, finely diced
½ tsp ground turmeric
1 garlic clove, crushed (or ½ tsp garlic purée)
250g basmati rice
500ml hot chicken or vegetable stock
75g frozen peas, thawed
Pinch of salt
1 bay leaf
1 piece of cinnamon stick
2 cardamom pods, split

This dish can be baked at a higher temperature for a shorter time (for when cooking the Tandoori Chicken, for example) or at a lower temperature for longer (when cooking other curries or casseroles in the oven).

- Preheat the oven to 220°C/gas 7 or 180°C/gas 4, depending on what else you are baking.

- Heat the oil in a flameproof casserole and fry the onion, carrots and pepper gently, stirring, for 4 minutes until softened but not browned.

- Stir in the turmeric, garlic and rice until all the grains are glistening.

- Add the stock, peas, salt, bay leaf and spices. Bring to the boil, stir, then cover and cook in the oven for 20 minutes at the higher temperature or 30 minutes at the lower temperature until the rice is just tender and the liquid is almost absorbed.

- Remove from the oven but do not uncover. Leave to stand for 10 minutes.

- Fluff up with a fork. Remove the bay leaf and spices, if liked, before serving.

• From the Curry House

Makes about 8 breads

Quick Naan Bread

Preparation time:
15 minutes
Cooking time:
8 minutes
To freeze:
Leave to cool, place in a
sealable freezer bag and freeze
for up to 6 months

I thought it was worth including this in case you forget to buy some naan bread when you're at the supermarket. It's very quick to prepare, light and delicious, so useful to make anytime there isn't any bread in the house!

- Mix all the ingredients except the cumin seeds together to form a soft dough.

- Knead gently on a lightly floured surface until smooth, then divide the mixture into 8 balls.

- Preheat the oven to 220°C/gas 7.

- Roll out to rounds about the size of your hand and pull one edge to make them pear-shaped.

- Place on non-stick baking sheets and brush with a little water. Sprinkle with the cumin seeds, if using, and press lightly into the surface.

- Bake in the oven for about 8 minutes until puffy and browning slightly.

- Wrap in a clean napkin until ready to serve. Serve warm.

250g self-raising flour
175ml plain yoghurt
1½ tbsp sunflower oil
½ tsp caster sugar
½ tsp salt
1 egg, beaten
1 tbsp cumin seeds
  (optional)

From the Chinese Takeaway

All the favourite classics like sweet and sour pork, chicken chow mein, Chinese spare ribs, egg foo yung and Peking duck are here, plus accompaniments such as crispy seaweed and spring rolls. Many of them are very quick to prepare. Keep dried noodles in the cupboard but when you can, fresh egg noodles from the supermarket chiller cabinet (usually next to the beansprouts) have a much better flavour and texture. Packs of ready-prepared stir-fry vegetables are good value, as are bags of beansprouts. Both can be frozen straight away in the packets they come in (useful if you buy them at reduced price for quick sale and don't want to eat them that day). They'll be fine for up to a month and, although a little flabby when thawed, as they are being thrown straight into a stir-fry (you can cook them from frozen), they're absolutely fine. Cans of bamboo shoots and water chestnuts are also great storecupboard standbys along with a jar of Chinese five-spice powder and a couple of the basic sauces – hoisin and oyster. Dark soy sauce is a must – did you know it's great for colouring gravy made with the meat pan juices when you cook a Sunday roast or classic beef casserole?

Takeaway Tip

Ready-to-eat rice: Boil twice as much rice as you need when serving it plain, cool it quickly (never leave cooked rice hanging around in a warm kitchen – it's a haven for bacteria that could cause food poisoning), then freeze it in sealable freezer bags. To defrost, pour boiling water over it, break it up, drain it well and use for egg fried rice (page 59).

Preparation time:
5 minutes

Cooking time:
6 minutes

To freeze:
Freeze before thickening with cornflour; cool quickly and freeze in a rigid container for up to 6 months; thaw, bring to the boil, then thicken as in the recipe

1 skinless chicken breast
900ml chicken stock
400g can creamed sweetcorn
½ tsp clear honey
4 tbsp cornflour
6 tbsp water
Salt and freshly ground black
   pepper

To garnish
1 spring onion, cut into
   short lengths and finely
   shredded or a few chive
   stalks (optional)

Serves 4

Chicken and Sweetcorn Soup

Everyone's favourite Chinese soup (particularly the kids) this is simple to make at home. You can use plain canned corn and mash it with a potato masher but you'll need to slightly increase the cornflour and water to thicken the soup.

• Finely chop the chicken breast (use a food processor if you have one). Tip into a saucepan.

• Stir in the stock and then add the sweetcorn and honey. Bring to the boil, then reduce the heat and simmer for 5 minutes.

• Blend the cornflour with the water and stir into the soup. Bring to the boil, stirring until thickened. Simmer for 1 minute more. Season to taste.

• Ladle into warm bowls and garnish with the shredded spring onion or a few chive stalks, if using.

• From the Chinese Takeaway

Serves 5

Wonton Soup

Preparation time:
20 minutes
Cooking time:
5 minutes
To freeze:
The filled dumplings can be
frozen uncooked for up to 3
months; place a little apart in a
rigid container, interleaved with
clingfilm if adding a second layer;
thaw before boiling in the stock

This delicious soup has little pork dumplings and vegetables so is a light meal all on its own! You can buy the wonton wrappers in Asian supermarkets or use my 'cheat' way below. Vary the flavour by using minced beef or chicken instead of pork, or a drained can of tuna.

For the soup
4 heaped tbsp dried sliced
   shiitake mushrooms
1.2 litres chicken stock
1 large head pak choi, finely
   shredded
2 tbsp sherry or rice wine
1 tsp clear honey
2 tsp soy sauce

For the wontons
200g minced pork
2 garlic cloves, crushed (or
   1 tsp garlic purée)
1 tsp grated fresh root
   ginger (or ginger purée)
2 tbsp soy sauce
4 large sheets filo pastry (or
   30 wonton wrappers)
1 egg, beaten (if using filo)

- Put the mushrooms in a large pan with the stock. Leave to soak while preparing the wontons.

- For the wonton filling, mix together the pork with the garlic, ginger and soy sauce.

- If using filo, lay 1 sheet of pastry on a board and brush all over the surface with beaten egg. Lay the second sheet on top and brush again. Cut into 15 equal squares (they should be about 8 cm^2). Repeat with the other 2 sheets. Divide the filling between the squares, putting towards one corner. Fold that corner up over the filling. Start to roll, then fold in the sides and roll up. Repeat with all the dumplings.

- If using wonton wrappers, fill and roll the same way but lay out one at a time and keep the unfilled and filled wontons covered with a damp cloth all the time as you work.

- Bring the chicken stock to the boil, drop in the dumplings and cook for 3 minutes. Add the shredded greens, sherry or rice wine, honey and soy sauce, stir gently, bring back to the boil and cook for a further 1 minute.

- Ladle into warm bowls and serve hot.

Preparation time:
10 minutes plus soaking time
Cooking time:
10 minutes
To freeze:
The omelette isn't suitable for freezing but any fresh remaining beansprouts can be frozen in a sealable freezer bag for up to 1 month

2 heaped tbsp dried sliced shiitake mushrooms or 4 fresh mushrooms, sliced
4 tbsp sunflower oil
75g cooked roast pork, thinly sliced and shredded
75g thawed frozen or cooked peas
4 small handfuls of fresh, or a drained can of beansprouts
2 spring onions, chopped (or a small handful of frozen chopped onion)
Handful of fresh spinach, or 1 small pak choi, or 3–4 Chinese leaves, or any other greens, shredded
6 eggs, beaten
1 tbsp soy sauce
½ tsp Chinese five-spice powder

To serve
Plain rice and a large salad

Serves 4

Egg Foo Yung

A Chinese omelette is a great way to use up any leftovers such as cooked chicken or vegetables or to add anything you fancy from a handful of cooked, peeled prawns, to some chopped ham or a drained can of sweetcorn.

Speed tip: Make 1 large omelette and cut it in quarters

- If using dried mushrooms, soak them in hot water for 30 minutes then drain before use.

- Heat 2 tbsp of the oil in a wok or large frying pan and stir-fry the pork, mushrooms and vegetables for 2 minutes.

- Tip into a bowl and mix in the beaten eggs and add the soy sauce and five-spice powder.

- Heat ½ tbsp of the remaining sunflower oil in an omelette pan. Add a quarter of the mixture and spread out evenly. Fry for 1–2 minutes until almost set, lifting the edge and tilting the pan so the runny egg flows underneath.

- Loosen and carefully fold the omelette in half. Slide out onto a warm plate. Keep warm whilst cooking the remaining omelettes in the same way.

- Serve hot with plain rice, and a large salad dressed with sunflower oil, orange juice and soy sauce. Good served cold in bread rolls or pittas for lunch too.

• From the Chinese Takeaway

Serves 4

Sweet and Sour Pork

Preparation time:
10 minutes
Cooking time:
12 minutes
To freeze:
Don't thicken with cornflour if
freezing but cool quickly, pack
in a rigid container and freeze
for up to 3 months; reheat, then
thicken before serving

You can do the same recipe with pieces of chicken breast or thigh, or chunks of skinned meaty white fish fillet. If you use fish, don't stir-fry the fish first, simply add after the soy sauce. Take care when thickening, too, not to break up the fish.

- Heat the oil in a wok or large frying pan. Add the pork and stir-fry for 4 minutes. Remove from the pan.

- Add the vegetables and stir-fry for 1 minute until they start to soften.

- Stir in the remaining ingredients except the cornflour and water, bring to the boil, then reduce the heat and simmer for 5 minutes.

- Return the pork to the pan.

- Blend the cornflour with the water and stir in. Bring to the boil and cook for 1 minute, stirring gently, until thickened slightly and clear. Taste and add more soy sauce, if liked.

- Serve with egg fried rice.

2 tbsp sunflower oil
500g pork stir-fry meat or
   fillet, cut into small strips
1 large carrot, cut into
   matchsticks
¼ cucumber, cut into
   matchsticks
1 red pepper, cut into thin
   strips
430g can of pineapple pieces
   in natural juice
2 tbsp tomato purée
4 tbsp soy sauce
1 tsp grated fresh root
   ginger (or ginger purée)
1 garlic clove, crushed (or
   ½ tsp garlic purée)
2 tbsp soft light brown sugar
2 tbsp rice or white wine
   vinegar
2 tsp cornflour
1 tbsp water

To serve
Egg Fried Rice (page 59)

Preparation time:
5 minutes
Cooking time:
1 hour 40 minutes
To freeze:
Cool quickly, pack in rigid containers or a sealable freezer bag and freeze for up to 2 months

700g Chinese spare ribs
2 tbsp malt or wine vinegar
1 tbsp sunflower oil
2 tsp grated fresh root ginger (or ginger purée)
2 tsp Chinese five spice powder
3 garlic cloves, crushed (or 1 ½ tsp garlic purée)
3 tbsp clear honey
4 tbsp soy sauce

Serves 4

Chinese Spare Ribs

If you try these and love them as much as I do, make loads and freeze them. The cooking time and effort is just the same for twice the quantity (as long as you have a large enough saucepan to cook them in).

- Place the ribs in a large pan and cover with water. Add the vinegar. Bring to the boil, then reduce the heat, cover and simmer gently for 1 hour.

- Preheat the oven to 180°C/gas 4. Dampen a roasting tin and line with non-stick baking parchment, making sure it comes up the sides of the tin (to prevent the glaze sticking to the tin – easier washing up!).

- Mix together all the remaining ingredients. Pour over the ribs and toss to coat completely in the sauce.

- Arrange the ribs in the prepared tin in a single layer. Spoon over any remaining sauce.

- Roast in the oven for about 40 minutes, turning once, until meltingly tender and stickily glazed. Serve hot.

To slow cook:
Mix the raw ribs in all the coating ingredients. Place in large slow cooker lined with baking parchment, and cook on LOW for 6–8 hours until meltingly tender, turning and rearranging once

To pressure cook:
Instead of step 1, pressure cook the ribs on HIGH pressure for 10 minutes, then reduce the pressure quickly under cold water, drain thoroughly and return to the saucepan, then continue to follow the recipe

• From the Chinese Takeaway

Serves 4

Chinese Chicken Curry

Preparation time:
5 minutes
Cooking time:
15 minutes
To freeze:
Don't thicken before freezing; cool quickly, pack in rigid containers and freeze for up to 3 months; thaw, bring to the boil and then thicken as in the recipe

This curry sauce is also popular served with chips. Simply thicken it with the blended cornflour at the end of the first step without adding the chicken. But as chips are not the healthiest option, perhaps you could try it with Golden Oven Wedges (page 111).

- Heat the oil in a wok or saucepan. Fry the onions and garlic, stirring, for 3–4 minutes until soft and lightly golden.

- Stir in the curry powder and fry for a further 30 seconds.

- Add the stock, honey and soy sauce and stir well, then add the chicken pieces.

- Bring to the boil, then reduce the heat, cover and simmer gently for 10 minutes until the chicken is tender and cooked through.

- Blend the cornflour with the water and stir into the chicken. Bring to the boil, stirring, then simmer 1 minute. Taste and add more soy sauce if necessary.

- Serve hot spooned over plain rice in bowls with the quick vegetable stir-fry.

2 tbsp sunflower oil
2 onions, chopped (or
    2 large handfuls of frozen
    chopped onions)
3 garlic cloves, crushed (or
    1½ tsp garlic purée)
1 tbsp curry powder
300ml chicken stock
2 tsp clear honey
3 tbsp soy sauce
500g diced skinless chicken
    breast (or 4 small chicken
    breasts, diced)
2 tbsp cornflour
2 tbsp water

To serve
    Plain rice and Quick
    Vegetable Stir-fry
(page 60)

Preparation time:
15 minutes
Cooking time:
8 minutes
To freeze:
Best eaten fresh, but you can freeze the other half of the packet of beansprouts in a sealable freezer bag for up to a month for use next time

3 slabs dried medium
  Chinese egg noodles
1 tsp toasted sesame oil (or
  sunflower oil)
2 tbsp sunflower oil
350g chicken stir-fry meat
  (or 3 small skinless breasts
  cut into thin strips)
1 red pepper, thinly sliced
1 green pepper, thinly sliced
100g mangetout, trimmed
½ bunch of spring onions,
  cut into large diagonal
  slices
½ packet fresh beansprouts
  (or a drained 400g can)
3 tbsp dark soy sauce
120ml chicken stock or
  water
1 tsp Chinese five-spice
  powder
Pinch of chilli powder
1 tbsp cornflour
1 tbsp water

Serves 4

Chicken Chow Mein

This is a quick and simple supper dish for all the family. There is no standard recipe. Use stir-fry pork instead of chicken if you prefer, and frozen peas can replace the mangetout for economy. This is also good with some sweet chilli sauce drizzled over for serving.

Speed tip: Use a 350g bag of ready-prepared stir-fry vegetables instead of the peppers, spring onions, mangetout and beansprouts

- Cook the noodles according to the packet directions. Drain, return to the saucepan or bowl and toss in the teaspoon of sesame or sunflower oil. Set aside.

- Heat the oil in a wok or large frying pan. Add the chicken and stir-fry for 3 minutes.

- Add the peppers, mangetout and spring onions and stir-fry a further 2 minutes.

- Add the beansprouts, soy sauce, stock or water and the spices and cook, stirring, for 1 minute.

- Blend the cornflour with the water and stir in. Cook for a further 1 minute.

- Stir in the noodles and heat through, tossing and stirring. Pile into bowls and serve hot.

• From the Chinese Takeaway

Serves 4

Peking Duck

Preparation time:
30 minutes
Cooking time:
2 hours
To freeze:
Cool quickly, then place the shredded duck in a sealable freezer bag and freeze for up to 6 months

Frozen ducks are normally cheaper than fresh but look out for fresh ones on offer (perhaps reduced for quick sale) or duck crowns are also often a good buy (not that much less meat). The pancakes are available from some supermarkets and Asian food stores.

1 fresh or thawed frozen oven-ready duckling, about 1kg
Salt
2 tbsp clear honey
1 tbsp soy sauce
20 Chinese pancakes

To serve
½ cucumber, cut into matchsticks; 1 bunch of spring onions, cut into short, fine shreds; hoisin sauce; and Beansprout and Pepper Salad (page 61)

> **Speed tip:** Try rolling the duck in flour tortillas – easier to find, much less fiddly and they taste just as delicious!

- Prick the duck all over with a fork. Place in a large container and pour a kettle of boiling water over it. Leave to stand for 5 minutes, then drain thoroughly. When cool enough, dry thoroughly inside and out with kitchen paper and season with salt.

- Preheat the oven to 230°C/gas 8. Place the duck on a rack in a roasting tin. Mix the honey with the soy sauce. Smear all over the duck, including the underside.

- Place the bird in the oven and roast for 15 minutes until the skin is beginning to crisp. Turn down the oven temperature to 160°C/gas 3 and cook for a further 1¾ hours.

- When the duck is cooked, carefully remove the dark, slightly crispy skin and cut into neat pieces. Cut all the meat off the bones, then shred between two forks.

- For each pancake, spread with a little hoisin sauce, add some duck, a piece of the soy and honey skin, some spring onion and cucumber, roll up and enjoy.

Cook's tip: Use the bones to make duck soup. Simply simmer them in light chicken stock for an hour. Strain, pick any meat off the bones and add, season with soy sauce and add some sliced mushrooms or peas and a good splash of sherry or rice wine. Thicken slightly with cornflour.

Preparation time:
10 minutes

Cooking time:
4 minutes

To freeze:
Best eaten fresh but can be
frozen in rigid containers for up
to 3 months

400g frying steak
4 tbsp soy sauce
3 tbsp sunflower oil
1 bunch of spring onions,
    cut in thirds then thin
    strips
125g oyster mushrooms,
    trimmed and halved if
    large
4 tbsp sherry or rice wine
4 tbsp oyster sauce
2 tsp grated fresh root
    ginger (or ginger purée)
1½ tbsp cornflour
150ml water

To serve
Plain rice and a Beansprout
    and Pepper Salad (page
    61)

Serves 4

Beef with Mushrooms and Oyster Sauce

You can use ordinary cup mushrooms instead of the oyster ones, if you prefer. Expensive fillet steak is another alternative but frying steak does just as well as long as you take the time to cut it in very thin, even strips.

- Using a sharp knife, cut the steak into very thin slices across the grain. Place in a shallow dish and sprinkle with half the soy sauce.

- Heat 2 tbsp of the oil in a wok or large frying pan. Separate the steak slices and drop into the hot wok. Stir-fry for 30 seconds until they just turn colour, then quickly remove from the pan with a slotted spoon.

- Add the remaining oil and heat. Reserve a few strips of spring onion for garnish. Stir-fry the remainder with the oyster mushrooms for 1 minute.

- Add the remaining soy sauce and the rest of the ingredients, except the cornflour and water, and stir briefly.

- Blend the cornflour with the water and stir in until thickened slightly. Return the beef and juices to the wok and toss gently until piping hot.

- Serve spooned over rice and garnished with the reserved spring onion shreds and accompany with the beansprout salad.

• From the Chinese Takeaway

Serves 4

Ginger Beef with Mangetout

Preparation time:
10 minutes

Cooking time:
5 minutes

To freeze:
The noodles are best prepared fresh: cool the meat quickly, pack in useable portions in rigid containers and freeze for up to 3 months

Thin frying steak is fine for this dish but make sure you cut it into very thin strips. You can, of course, use more expensive rump or fillet if you prefer. Thawed, frozen cut green beans can be used in place of the mangetout.

- Cook the noodles according to the packet directions.

- Meanwhile, put the meat in a shallow dish. Add the ginger, garlic and cornflour and mix together thoroughly.

- Heat the oil in a wok or large frying pan. Separate the strips of steak, add to the wok, and stir-fry quickly for 1 minute.

- Add the mangetout and stir-fry a further 1 minute.

- Add the honey, water, sherry or rice wine and soy sauce and toss until slightly thickened and the sauce is clear.

- Drain the noodles, toss in the sesame or sunflower oil and 1 tbsp of the sesame seeds.

- Pile in bowls and top with the ginger beef. Sprinkle with the remaining sesame seeds to garnish.

4 slabs dried medium
   Chinese egg noodles
350g thin frying steak, cut
   into very thin strips
1 tbsp grated fresh root
   ginger (or ginger purée)
1 garlic clove, crushed (or
   $\frac{1}{2}$ tsp garlic purée)
1 tbsp cornflour
2 tbsp sunflower oil
200g mangetout, trimmed
1$\frac{1}{2}$ tsp clear honey
150ml water
1 tbsp sherry or rice wine
2 tbsp soy sauce
1 tbsp sesame oil (or
   sunflower oil)
2 tbsp sesame seeds

Preparation time:
10 minutes
Cooking time:
5 minutes
To freeze:
Best eaten fresh

Serves 4

Prawns with Cashew Nuts

3 tbsp sunflower oil
1 bunch of spring onions,
   trimmed and cut into
   short lengths
150g button mushrooms,
   sliced
½ cucumber, cut into
   matchsticks
400g beansprouts
100g raw cashew nuts
300g raw peeled tiger
   prawns
2 tbsp dark or light soy
   sauce
2 tsp lemon juice

To serve
Plain rice or egg noodles

This is really quick to make. For an inexpensive mid-week version, use a pack of seafood sticks, cut into small chunks, instead of the prawns, and raw peanuts instead of cashews. The cucumber gives it an excellent texture and subtle flavour.

- Heat the oil in a wok or large saucepan. Add the spring onions and stir-fry for 1 minute.

- Add the mushrooms and cucumber and stir-fry a further 1 minute.

- Add the beansprouts, nuts and prawns and stir-fry for about 2 minutes until the prawns are pink.

- Stir in the soy sauce and lemon juice and toss quickly.

- Serve hot, spooned over plain rice or egg noodles.

• From the Chinese Takeaway

Makes 16

Prawn Toasts

Preparation time:
10 minutes
Cooking time:
4–6 minutes
To freeze:
Best eaten fresh

These are quick to make and are delicious served with drinks or as a starter to any Chinese meal. The knack is to have the oil good and hot so the toasts sizzle and brown quickly and don't absorb too much oil. Use a small food processor to chop the prawns if you have one.

- Mix the prawns with the ginger, garlic, soy sauce, sesame oil and egg white. Spread on the bread, right out to the edges. Sprinkle liberally with the sesame seeds and press down well. Cut one each in 4 triangles.

- Heat about 1cm sunflower oil in a deep frying pan until a few sesame seeds dropped in sizzle furiously and rise to the surface.

- Add half the toasts, prawn-sides up, and fry for 2–3 minutes until golden, pressing them down gently into the oil with a fish slice to set the tops. Remove with a fish slice and drain on kitchen paper. Keep them warm whilst you cook the remaining toasts. Drain in the same way.

- Serve warm with sweet chilli dipping sauce.

300g cooked peeled prawns, thawed if frozen, and finely chopped
2 tsp grated fresh root ginger (or ginger purée)
1 garlic clove, crushed (or ½ tsp garlic purée)
2 tsp cornflour
2 tsp light soy sauce
2 tsp sesame oil
1 egg white, lightly beaten
4 slices white bread from a large sliced loaf
2 tbsp sesame seeds
Sunflower oil for frying

To serve
Sweet chilli sauce

Preparation time:
10 minutes
Cooking time:
5 minutes
To freeze:
Not suitable for freezing

Serves 4

Szechuan Spicy Peanut Noodles with Vegetables

4 slabs dried medium egg
  noodles
2 tbsp sunflower oil
2 garlic cloves, crushed (or
  1 tsp garlic purée)
1 tsp grated fresh root
  ginger (or ginger purée)
1 tsp dried chilli flakes
4 tbsp crunchy peanut
  butter
2 tbsp soy sauce
1 tbsp clear honey
1 tbsp lime juice
4 tbsp water
4 spring onions, chopped
1 red or green pepper, finely
  diced
½ cucumber, finely diced
8 radishes, sliced

To serve
Green salad

These are quick and simple to make. They taste good cold for lunch too. You can add any other veggies that take your fancy but these give a great flavour and a nice bit of crunch. If eating cold, stir in a dash of cold water to thin the sauce slightly as it firms on cooling.

- Cook the noodles according to the packet directions. Drain thoroughly.

- Heat the oil in a wok or large saucepan. Add the garlic, ginger and chilli flakes and fry gently for 30 seconds.

- Stir in the peanut butter, soy sauce, honey, lime juice and water. Stir until combined to a sauce and gently bubbling.

- Add the noodles and prepared vegetables. Toss gently but thoroughly until heated through.

- Serve in bowls with a crisp green salad.

• From the Chinese Takeaway

Serves 4

Egg Fried Rice

Preparation time:
5 minutes
Cooking time:
15 minutes (including rice cooking)
To freeze:
Best eaten fresh as the egg will go a bit rubbery in the freezer, although it can be frozen for up to 3 months

Turn this into Special Fried Rice by adding a handful each of cooked, peeled prawns and finely diced, cooked chicken or pork to the rice before stirring in the egg. Or add sweetcorn, cooked green beans or sliced mushrooms. Use cooked leftover rice if you have it.

- Cook the rice in boiling, salted water according to the packet directions, adding the peas for the last 5 minutes of cooking. Drain thoroughly.

- Heat the oil in a large frying pan or wok. Add the rice and toss until glistening and all the grains are separate.

- Push the rice to one side of the pan. Pour the egg onto the empty side of the pan. Cook, stirring and gradually drawing in the rice, until strands of egg are incorporated through it.

- Sprinkle the five-spice powder and splash of soy sauce over and toss thoroughly. Serve hot.

225g basmati or other long-grain rice
Salt
100g frozen peas
2 tbsp sunflower oil
1 egg, beaten
¼ tsp Chinese five-spice powder
A splash of soy sauce

Preparation time:
2 minutes
Cooking time:
5 minutes
To freeze:
Best eaten fresh

Serves 4

Quick Vegetable Stir-fry

2 tbsp sunflower oil
350–450g bag fresh or
   frozen ready-prepared
   stir-fry vegetables
1 garlic clove, crushed (or
   ½ tsp garlic purée)
1 tsp grated fresh root
   ginger (or ginger purée)
2 tsp clear honey
3 tbsp soy sauce
1 tbsp sherry or rice wine (or
   orange juice)

Turn this into a quick meal by adding two or three blocks of
cooked, dried Chinese egg noodles and a couple of large handfuls
of peanuts or cashews, or a large, drained can of soya beans. Shred
your own raw vegetables like cabbage, peppers and onions if you
prefer.

- Heat the oil in a wok. Add the vegetables and stir-fry for
  3 minutes until slightly softened.

- Add the remaining ingredients and stir fry for a further
  1–2 minutes. Serve hot.

• From the Chinese Takeaway

Serves 4

Preparation time:
5 minutes
To freeze:
Not suitable for freezing

Beansprout and Pepper Salad

This is crisp and light and makes a delicious accompaniment to any Chinese dish. Try it, too, with some grated carrot or celeriac added and a handful of raw peanuts or cashew nuts stirred through for a simple snack lunch or supper.

- Put the beansprouts, peppers and spring onions in a bowl.

- Whisk the remaining ingredients together and pour over. Toss well and chill for 20 minutes, if time, to allow the flavours to develop.

200g fresh beansprouts
2 red or green peppers, cut into thin strips
2 spring onions, chopped
2 tbsp sunflower oil
1 tbsp dark or light soy sauce
1 tbsp pure orange juice
½ tsp Chinese five-spice powder

Preparation time:
30 minutes
Cooking time:
15–20 minutes
To freeze:
Best eaten fresh, but can be
cooked then frozen if you use
peas, not prawns; thaw before
reheating in a hot oven

Makes 8

Spring Rolls

1 tbsp soy sauce
1 tsp clear honey
2 spring onions, chopped
1 small carrot, grated
4 button mushrooms, sliced
Large handful of fresh
  beansprouts
Handful of cooked, peeled
  prawns, or peas, thawed if
  frozen
$\frac{1}{4}$ tsp Chinese five-spice
  powder
$1\frac{1}{2}$ tsp cornflour
8 small or 4 large filo pastry
  sheets
A little sunflower oil

These are usually deep-fried but taste delicious baked in the oven, have far fewer calories and are less greasy. Ring the changes with some chopped tofu or cold roast pork instead of the prawns or peas. If you wish, you can deep-fry them in hot sunflower oil until golden.

- Mix together the soy sauce and honey until blended, then stir in everything else except the pastry and oil.

- Preheat the oven to 200°C/gas 6 and oil a baking sheet with sunflower oil.

- If using large filo sheets, cut them in half to make 2 squares before you start. Fold each square in half. Divide the filling between them, putting it in the centre along one short edge. Brush the pastry edges with water. Fold in the sides, then roll up.

- Place the rolls on the prepared baking sheet and brush with a little more oil. Bake in the oven for 15–20 minutes until crisp and golden brown. Serve hot.

• From the Chinese Takeaway

Serves 4

Crispy Seaweed

Preparation time:
10 minutes
Cooking time:
2 minutes
To freeze:
Not suitable for freezing

This is, really, shredded spring greens but they taste great. Make sure you cut the greens very finely. The easiest way is to separate into leaves, cut out the thick stalk, roll up the leaves and cut across in very thin shreds. Don't overcook or they will go brown and bitter.

Sunflower oil, for frying
350g spring greens, finely
   shredded, discarding thick
   stalk
½ tsp Chinese five-spice
   powder
¼ tsp salt

- Heat about 1cm of oil in a deep frying pan until a cube of day-old bread browns in 30 seconds or until a few strands of the greens immediately rise to the surface sizzling furiously.

- Fry the shredded greens in small batches for about 20 seconds just until the sizzling stops and the 'seaweed' is bright green and crisp. Remove with a slotted spoon and drain on kitchen paper. Keep warm until all the greens are cooked. Reheat the oil between each batch.

- Mix the five-spice powder and salt together and sprinkle over. Toss gently and serve.

From the Pizza House

Takeaway pizzas are renowned for being very high in fat, salt, sugar and calories (they're also incredibly expensive if you have them delivered). Some supermarket frozen ones taste okay but they often have a sickly, slightly slimy tomato sauce base, which permeates the whole thing. Pizzas are fun to make (get the kids involved) and here you'll find thin-crust, deep-pan, filled-crust pizzas and calzones (stuffed pizzas) but you'll also find a couple of really quick recipes for when only pizza will do but time is too short to make yeast dough from scratch!

Pizza base mixes are a good alternative to my yeast dough. Another quick tip is to keep some good-quality stone-baked Margherita pizzas in the freezer, then add your own healthy and delicious toppings for a pizza feast.

Make sure you serve with a large Italian salad or perhaps some good-quality coleslaw (see page 106 for a great home-made one).

Takeaway Tip

Tomato base: If you don't have any passata to make a tomato base, you can just smear the pizza dough with a little tomato purée (not too much!) and sprinkle with a little dried basil or oregano.

CHAPTER 5

Preparation time:
10 minutes
Cooking time:
9–11 minutes
To freeze:
Best eaten fresh but can be
frozen; cool, then open-freeze
until firm, wrap in a sealable
plastic bag and store for up to 3
months

100g self-raising flour
1 tsp baking powder
¼ tsp salt
Freshly ground black pepper
4 tbsp olive oil
60ml cold water
3 tbsp tomato purée or
    passata
½ tsp dried oregano
75g Cheddar or Mozzarella
    cheese, grated
4 cherry tomatoes, sliced
    (optional)
A few stoned black olives
    (optional)

To garnish
A few torn fresh basil leaves
    (optional)

To serve
Large mixed salad

Makes a 23cm pizza

Quick Pan Pizza

Yeast pizza dough takes time as it has to rise, but this frying pan
version is a great quick and easy treat when you fancy a pizza in a
hurry. It's more substantial than the flat bread pizza on page 67.
Add other toppings of your choice.

- Sift together the flour, baking powder and salt. Add a good
  grinding of black pepper.

- Stir in 2 tbsp of the oil and enough of the cold water to form a
  soft but not sticky dough. Knead gently and roll out on a floured
  surface to about 23cm round (or the size of the base of your fairly
  large, non-stick frying pan).

- Heat a further 1 tbsp of oil in the pan. Swirl round to coat the
  base. Add the dough and fry over a moderate heat for 3–4
  minutes until golden. Don't have the heat too high or it will burn.

- Carefully slide the dough out of the pan onto a plate. Invert the
  pan over the plate then carefully tip the pizza base back into the
  pan, browned side up. Turn down the heat to low.

- Spread with the tomato purée or passata then sprinkle with the
  oregano. Add the cheese, then the sliced tomatoes and olives, if
  using. Drizzle with the remaining olive oil. Cover with foil or a lid
  and cook gently for 6–7 minutes until the cheese melts.

- Scatter the torn basil over, if using, cut into wedges and serve hot
  with a large mixed salad.

• From the Pizza House

Serves 4

Preparation time:
10 minutes
Cooking time:
6 minutes
To freeze:
Not suitable for freezing

Fast Flatbread Pizza

The perfect storecupboard standby for a quick lunch or supper, ring the changes with other ingredients. Try spreading the breads with a little tomato purée, some drained sweet pepper antipasti, Mozzarella slices, a drizzle of olive oil and some torn basil leaves.

- Preheat the oven to 200°C/gas 6.

- Lay the tortillas on 2 large baking sheets (or 4 individual ovenproof plates).

- Spread each one with a tablespoon of the tomato purée, then dot the caramelised onions in small blobs over the top.

- Squeeze the spinach well to remove excess moisture. Scatter over the onions in small clumps.

- Scatter over the beetroot and cheese, dust with the sage and a good grinding of black pepper.

- Drizzle with a little olive oil. Bake in the oven for about 6 minutes until the cheese is melting slightly and the edges are crisp. Slide onto plates and serve straight away.

4 flour tortillas or khobez (Mediterranean flatbreads)
4 tbsp tomato purée
4 tbsp caramelised onions from a jar
4 handfuls of frozen leaf spinach, thawed
2 cooked beetroot, diced
150g feta or goats' cheese, diced
1 tsp dried sage
Freshly ground black pepper
2 tbsp olive oil

Makes 2 large or 4 small pizzas

Basic Pizza Dough

450g strong plain flour
1 tsp salt
1 tsp caster sugar
2 tsp fast-action dried yeast
2 tbsp olive oil, plus extra
  for greasing
300ml lukewarm water

After the basic dough recipe, you'll find a range of toppings to transform it into your favourite takeaway TV dinner. If you have a breadmaker, set it to the dough programme, add the ingredients and let it do the work. For thicker pizzas, increase the quantity.

Speed tip: Use 2 large pizza base mixes instead of making your own from scratch and there's no need to let it rise before shaping

- Put the flour, salt and sugar in a bowl. Add the yeast, then the oil and water and mix to form a soft but not too sticky dough. Knead gently on a lightly floured surface for at least 5 minutes until smooth and elastic. Alternatively make the dough in a food processor with the dough hook fitted.

- Return the dough to the bowl, cover with oiled clingfilm and leave in a warm place until doubled in bulk – about 50 minutes.

- Preheat the oven to 220°C/gas 7. Place pizza plates or large baking sheets in the oven to heat.

- Re-knead the dough briefly, roll out on a lightly floured surface to four small rounds, about 20cm in diameter, or 2 large ones, around 30cm in diameter.

- Oil the hot pizza plates or baking sheets and put the dough on them, pressing out again to the size required. (A third option is to make two rectangular pizza bases in large, shallow oiled baking tins and serve them cut in squares.) Top with your chosen toppings (see following recipes) and bake according to the individual recipes, swapping the baking sheets over half way through cooking, if necessary, when making small pizzas.

• From the Pizza House

Makes 2 large or 4 small pizzas

Pizza Napolitana

Preparation time:
25 minutes plus rising
Cooking time:
20 minutes
To freeze:
Open-freeze the uncooked pizza until firm, then wrap and store in the freezer for up to 2 months

The traditional simple cheese and tomato pizza, you can add some sliced fresh tomatoes or a few chopped sun-dried ones to it as well if you like before adding the cheese. If you haven't any fresh basil, use 1 tsp dried basil.

- Shape the dough as in the basic recipe and preheat the oven to 220°C/gas 7.

- Mix together the tomato base ingredients and spread very thinly over the dough.

- Scatter the Mozzarella slices over, drizzle with olive oil and sprinkle with the basil leaves.

- Bake for 20 minutes or until the crust is golden and the cheese has melted and is lightly browning in places. Pile some rocket on top, if using.

1 quantity Basic Pizza Dough (page 68)

For the tomato base
6 tbsp passata
2 tbsp tomato purée
1 garlic clove, crushed (or ½ tsp garlic purée)
½ tsp caster sugar
Salt and freshly ground black pepper

For the topping
2 x 125g balls Mozzarella cheese, drained and sliced
1 tbsp olive oil
Handful of torn basil leaves

To garnish
A large handful of rocket leaves (optional)

Preparation time:
35 minutes plus rising
Cooking time:
20 minutes
To freeze:
Open-freeze the uncooked pizza
without the eggs, then wrap and
store in the freezer for up to
2 months

1 quantity Basic Pizza
   Dough (page 68)
Tomato base (see Pizza
   Napolitana topping, page
   69)
250g fresh or thawed frozen
   spinach
Freshly grated nutmeg
½ tsp dried oregano
Salt and freshly ground black
   pepper
50g soft blue cheese, pulled
   into tiny pieces
100g Mozzarella cheese,
   grated
4 smallish eggs
1 tbsp olive oil
1 tbsp fresh Parmesan
   shavings

Makes 2 large or 4 small pizzas

Pizza Fiorentina

Substitute small spoonfuls of soft white cheese instead of the blue, if
you prefer. If you make large pizzas, you can top them with little
quails eggs dotted all round the pizza instead of the hen's eggs, five
minutes before the end of cooking so everyone gets some egg.

- Shape the dough as in the basic recipe and preheat the oven to
  220°C/gas 7.

- If using fresh spinach, wash well, shake off any excess moisture
  and cook in a saucepan with no extra water for 3 minutes, stirring
  until wilted. Drain thoroughly and leave until cool enough to
  handle. Squeeze out any excess moisture from the spinach.

- Prepare the tomato base and spread thinly over the dough. Bake
  in the oven for 10 minutes.

- Remove from the oven, scatter the spinach over in small clumps
  and dust with the nutmeg and oregano. Season lightly. Scatter the
  small pieces of blue cheese and the Mozzarella over the spinach.
  Make a small well in the centre of each small pizza or on each
  half of a large one. Break an egg into each. Drizzle with the olive
  oil. Return to the oven for 10 minutes or until the crust is golden
  and the eggs are cooked to your liking. Sprinkle with the
  Parmesan and serve.

• From the Pizza House

Makes 2 large or 4 small pizzas

Spicy Meat Feast Pizza

Preparation time:
35 minutes plus rising

Cooking time:
20 minutes

To freeze:
Open-freeze the uncooked pizza without the eggs, then wrap and store in the freezer for up to 2 months

You can vary the heat by increasing or reducing the chilli according to taste. Use minced lamb instead of beef or, for something different, try skinning and crumbling a couple of pork sausages instead of the minced meat.

- Shape the dough as in the basic recipe and preheat the oven to 220°C/gas 7.

- Heat 1 tbsp of the oil in a small saucepan. Add the beef, onion and pepper and fry, stirring, until the grains of meat are separate and no longer pink.

- Add the chilli flakes and cook, stirring, for a further 1 minute.

- Add the tomato purée, sugar and some salt and pepper.

- Prepare the tomato base and spread thinly over the pizzas. Scatter the meat mixture over, then the diced chorizo or sausage. Scatter a few slices of jalapeño on top.

- Sprinkle over the cheese and add a few olives, if using. Drizzle with the remaining olive oil and bake in the oven for about 20 minutes until the crust is crisp and golden and the cheese is melted and bubbling and lightly browned in places.

1 quantity Basic Pizza Dough (page 68)
2 tbsp olive oil
100g lean minced beef
1 small onion, grated (or 1 tsp onion granules or 2 tsp onion purée)
1 small red pepper, finely diced
1 tsp dried chilli flakes
1 tbsp tomato purée
Pinch of caster sugar
Salt and freshly ground black pepper
1 quantity tomato base (see Pizza Napolitana topping page 69)
70g diced chorizo, salami or pepperoni
A few slices of pickled jalapeño pepper
50g Mozzarella cheese, grated
A few black olives (optional)

Preparation time:
30 minutes plus rising

Cooking time:
20 minutes

To freeze:
Open-freeze the uncooked
pizza, then wrap and store in
the freezer for up to 2 months

Makes 2 large or 4 small pizzas

Four Seasons Pizza

1 quantity Basic Pizza
  Dough (page 68)
1 quantity tomato base (see
  Pizza Napolitana topping
  page 69)
3 tbsp grated Parmesan
  cheese
100g Mozzarella cheese,
  grated
1 jar sliced artichoke hearts
  in olive oil, drained,
  reserving the oil
4 slices pancetta, diced
4 cup mushrooms, sliced
8 black olives, stoned and
  halved
2 tsp pickled capers
1 tsp dried oregano
Salt and freshly ground black
  pepper

Most people think that this is known as four seasons – or *quattro
stagioni* – because the topping ingredients are divided into four
quarters on the pizza – but some think it's the ingredients that
represent the seasons.

- Shape the dough as in the basic recipe and preheat the oven to
  220°C/gas 7.

- Prepare the tomato base and spread thinly over the pizzas.
  Sprinkle the cheeses over. Arrange the artichokes, pancetta,
  mushrooms and olives over the four quarters of each pizza.
  Scatter the capers on top and sprinkle with the oregano and a
  little salt and pepper. Drizzle with 1 tbsp of the reserved artichoke
  olive oil.

- Bake in the oven for about 20 minutes until the crust is crisp and
  golden.

• From the Pizza House

Makes 2 deep pizzas

Deep-pan Filled Crust Pizza

Preparation time:
35 minutes plus rising

Cooking time:
30 minutes

To freeze:
Open-freeze the uncooked pizza until firm, then remove from the tins, if liked, wrap and store in the freezer for up to 2 months

You can omit the cheese filling in the crust for a classic deep-pan (and use a 25cm tin) and, of course, add any filling you like to this pizza but this is a popular combination. If you don't have deep, slanting-sided pie tin, flan dishes will do instead..

1 quantity Basic Pizza Dough (page 68)
200g Cheddar or Emmental cheese in a block
100g Mozzarella cheese, grated
2 tbsp passata
1/2 tsp dried basil
1/2 red pepper, thinly sliced
1/2 green pepper, thinly sliced
1/2 small red onion, thinly sliced
4 button mushrooms, sliced
2 rashers rindless streaky bacon, diced (or a handful diced pancetta)
Salt and freshly ground black pepper
1 tbsp olive oil

- Preheat the oven to 220°C/gas 7 and place 2 baking sheets in the oven to get hot.

- Re-knead the dough but don't shape as in the original recipe. Oil 2 large deep round pie tins, 23cm in diameter. Cut the dough in half, put in the tins and press out so it lines the bases and comes right up the sides of the tins and hangs over the edges.

- Brush the dough with water. Cut the cheese in 1cm thick slices, then cut each slice in half lengthways to form sticks. Place the sticks of cheese all round the edge of the dough in the base of the tins. Fold the dough edges over the cheese to cover completely and press firmly all round so the dough is sealed to the base and flattened as much as possible.

- Spread the passata in the bases of the pizzas and sprinkle with the basil. Top with the remaining ingredients and sprinkle with the grated Mozzarella. Season with just a pinch of salt but plenty of black pepper.

- Drizzle with the olive oil. Place the tins on the hot baking sheets and bake for about 30 minutes until risen, crisp and golden round the edges.

- Serve hot cut into wedges.

Preparation time:
30 minutes plus rising
Cooking time:
20 minutes
To freeze:
Open-freeze the uncooked calzone, then wrap and store in the freezer for up to 2 months

1 quantity Basic Pizza Dough (page 68)
50g butter
2 large garlic cloves, crushed (or 1 tsp garlic purée)
1 tbsp chopped fresh rosemary (or 1 tsp dried, crushed)
1 small can of anchovy fillets, drained
2 tbsp sliced stoned black olives
1 courgette, grated and excess moisture squeezed out
2 large tomatoes, chopped
100g ricotta (or other soft white cheese)
50g Mozzarella cheese, grated
50g soft blue cheese, cut into small pieces (or grated Cheddar)
Salt and freshly ground black pepper
2 tbsp olive oil

To serve
2 tbsp grated Parmesan cheese

Serves 4

Calzone

In this recipe, the dough is folded over the filling, encasing it rather like a pasty. Choose filling ingredients with lots of aroma – such as plenty of fresh herbs, garlic, seafood and so on, so you can enjoy the heady scent when you split it open.

• Roll out the dough and shape into 4 rounds, as in the basic recipe for 4 small pizzas, and preheat the oven to 220°C/gas 7.

• Mash the butter, garlic and rosemary together and spread over the four rounds of dough, leaving a 2cm border all round.

• Divide the remaining ingredients, except the seasoning and oil, over the top of each dough round, leaving the border clear. Season with just a tiny pinch or grinding of salt (the anchovies are salty) and plenty of pepper. Drizzle with half the oil.

• Brush the edges with water. Fold the pizzas in half and press the edges well together, then roll the edge over all around to seal. Transfer to an oiled baking sheet. Brush the tops with olive oil. Bake in the oven for about 20 minutes or until crisp and golden.

• Serve dusted with grated Parmesan.

• From the Pizza House

Preparation time:
25 minutes
Cooking time:
20 minutes
To freeze:
Best eaten fresh

What's in My Fridge Stuffed Pizza

I've given some examples of leftovers to use but be bold and experimental – use anything from beetroot to cooked carrots, bits of bacon (fry off first) to rocket, spinach or the odd chopped spring onion – the constants are the tomato base, herbs and cheese.

- Make up the dough according to the packet directions and roll out into 4 rounds as large as possible (take care not to make any holes).

- Preheat the oven to 220°C/gas 7.

- Spread the centres of the dough with a little tomato purée, leaving a wide border all round. Divide the cheese over the centres of the dough. Top with the remaining ingredients, seasoning well and drizzling with half the olive oil.

- Brush the edges with water and draw the dough up over the filling, like wrapping a parcel, so they are sealed completely. Repeat with all four rounds. Carefully transfer to an oiled baking sheet, folded-sides down.

- Brush with the remaining oil and bake in the oven for about 20 minutes until crisp and golden.

- Meanwhile heat the passata in a saucepan. Transfer the stuffed pizzas to warm plates. Spoon the passata over and sprinkle with the Parmesan.

2 x 290g pizza base mix (or 1 quantity Basic Pizza Dough (page 68))
2 tbsp tomato purée
4 handfuls of grated Mozzarella or Cheddar cheese
2 tomatoes, chopped
2 mushrooms, chopped
Handful of cooked peas, sweetcorn or chopped green beans
1 tbsp capers or sliced olives
2 slices cooked ham, chopped (or 4 tbsp canned tuna, cooked chicken, thawed frozen prawns, chorizo etc.)
4 good pinches dried oregano or basil
Salt and freshly ground black pepper
2 tbsp olive oil, plus extra for greasing

To serve
120ml passata
2 tbsp grated Parmesan cheese

Preparation time:
8 minutes
To freeze:
Not suitable for freezing

Serves 4

Italian Salad

1 little gem lettuce,
  shredded
2 large handfuls of rocket
1 red pepper, thinly sliced
1 green pepper, thinly sliced
8 cherry tomatoes, halved
1 small red onion, sliced into
  rings
8–12 black or green olives

For the dressing
3 tbsp olive oil
1 tbsp red wine vinegar
2 tsp clear honey
¼ tsp dried oregano
¼ tsp dried basil
¼ tsp dried thyme
Salt and freshly ground black
  pepper

This is a simple, large mixed salad but with a delicious herby dressing. Try adding a splash of passata to the dressing for added depth of flavour. For a touch of luxury, add a few sliced artichoke hearts in oil from a jar.

Speed tip: Slice the onion without peeling, then separate into rings, discarding the two outer layers.

- Put all the prepared salad ingredients in a salad bowl.

- Put the dressing ingredients in a small bowl and whisk until blended and emulsified.

- Pour over the salad, toss and serve.

• From the Pizza House

Makes 16

Dough Balls

Preparation time:
15 minutes plus rising
Cooking time:
10 minutes
To freeze:
Pack in a sealable freezer bag
and freeze for up to 6 months

These make a delicious starter on their own or with Parma ham and melon or figs, or a tricolour salad (tomatoes, mozzarella and rocket). For a dessert, omit the garlic oil, dust the cooked balls with icing sugar and serve with strawberries and warm chocolate spread to dip into.

½ quantity Basic Pizza
   Dough (page 68)
6 tbsp olive oil
4 garlic cloves, crushed (or
   2 tsp garlic purée)
Coarse sea salt

- Make the dough as on page 68 and leave to rise. Knock back and shape into 16 small balls. Place a little apart on an oiled baking sheet. Leave in a warm place to rise again for 20–30 minutes.

- Preheat the oven to 220°C/gas 7.

- Whisk together the olive oil and garlic. Brush all over the balls. Bake in the oven for about 10 minutes until pale golden and cooked through (the base should sound hollow when tapped).

- Brush again with the rest of the garlic mixture until it is absorbed, then sprinkle with coarse sea salt. Serve whilst still warm.

From the Chippy

Fish 'n' chips is the traditional British takeaway and there's nothing like it when it's cooked well. Unfortunately, that's not always the case. It can be really greasy with soft batter and soggy chips – horrible! That happens because the oil has not been heated to the correct temperature – it must be really hot or it is absorbed by the food instead of just sealing the outside. Also, if the same oil has been used too often, the polyunsaturated fats turn into trans fats, which are known to be bad for us; it also then has a lower smoking point so won't get hot enough to cook the food correctly. So, although you can store your oil to use to deep-fry more than once, you must not use it more than three times. If you see it is starting to solidify in the bottle you *know* it's turned! But, having said all that, let's get back to the food.

You can't beat good fish and chips, so here we celebrate them and show you how to make perfect crunchy, light batter (and a beer batter for those special occasions) and chips that are fluffy on the inside but crisp and golden on the outside. You can also try a lovely crumb-coated oven version and excellent fresh-tasting mushy peas – there's even some quick pickled eggs, just for fun! The traditional accompaniments are, of course, ketchup and malt vinegar but fish and chips are also delicious with the other classic sauce for fish – tartare – so there's a simple version of that too (though you can, of course, buy some good-quality ones in the supermarket).

Takeaway Tip

Skinning fish: To skin fish, make a cut between the skin and the flesh at the tail end, keeping the knife close to the skin. Dip your fingers of the other hand in salt to grip the flap of skin. Keeping it taut, saw and push the knife along the fillet, separating flesh from skin.

Preparation time:
20 minutes
Cooking time:
14 minutes
To freeze:
Best eaten fresh

Serves 4

Classic Battered Fish and Chips

4 large potatoes
Sunflower oil
4 x 150g pieces pollock fillet
(or other sustainable
white fish), skinned, if
liked
2 tbsp plain or self-raising
flour
Salt and freshly ground black
pepper

For the batter
100g self-raising flour
Good pinch of salt
150ml very cold water

To serve
Mushy Peas (page 85) or
garden peas, vinegar or
lemon juice, ketchup
and/or Quick Tartare
Sauce (page 87)

I use pollock for my fish and chips because it's inexpensive and sustainable. You can, of course, use any white fish – just check that it has be responsibly fished – it should be clearly shown on fishmonger tags (or ask your fishmonger) or on the packaging.

Speed tip: Use ready-prepared, low-fat oven chips instead of making your own

- Peel the potatoes, cut in 5–6 slices lengthways, then cut each slice into chips. Place in a pan of water. Bring to the boil and boil for 2 minutes. Drain and dry thoroughly in a clean cloth.

- Heat about 1cm sunflower oil in a large, deep frying pan until very hot and a chip sizzles and rises to the surface immediately (or heat oil in a deep-fat fryer to 190°C).

- Carefully slide half the chips into the oil and fry for about 6 minutes, turning occasionally until crisp and golden. Drain on kitchen paper. Keep warm while cooking the remainder.

- Meanwhile wipe the fish. Mix the 2 tbsp flour with a little salt and pepper. Use to coat the fish.

- To make the batter, mix the flour and salt in a bowl. Whisk in the water to form a thick cream.

- Whilst the second batch of chips is cooking, heat about 1cm sunflower oil in a separate, large frying pan until a tip of a teaspoonful of the batter dropped in sizzles and rises to the surface immediately.

• From the Chippy

- Quickly dip the fish in the batter on both sides. Drain off the excess. Lay the fish in the pan and cook for about 2 minutes until golden underneath. Turn the fish over and fry the other side for a further 2 minutes until crisp and golden all over. Remove with a fish slice and drain on kitchen paper.

- Serve the fish and chips with mushy or plain peas, vinegar or lemon juice, and tomato ketchup and/or tartare sauce.

Cook's tip: For Beer-battered Fish, substitute lager or light ale for the water and fold in a stiffly beaten egg white.

Preparation time:
15 minutes
Cooking time:
30 minutes
To freeze:
Best eaten fresh

Serves 4

Oven-baked Crumb-coated Fish and Chips

4 large potatoes
2 tbsp sunflower oil
4 x 150g pieces sustainable
    white fish fillet, skinned
2 tbsp plain flour
Salt and freshly ground black
    pepper
1 egg, beaten
100g natural dried
    breadcrumbs

To serve
Mushy Peas (page 85) or
    garden peas and Quick
    Tartare Sauce (page 87)

These oven-baked fish and chips are ideal when you don't want to smell of frying. Another advantage is that they are a healthier option than the traditional recipe. You can leave them to cook whilst you go and have a shower or watch your favourite programme.

Speed tip: Use frozen chips for frying (not oven chips) instead of preparing your own

- Preheat the oven to 220°C/gas 7.

- Peel the potatoes, cut in 5 slices lengthways, then cut each slice into chips. Place in a bowl, add the oil and toss to coat. Lift out of the bowl, so any excess oil drains off, and transfer to a baking sheet.

- Wipe the fish. Mix the flour with a little salt and pepper on one plate. Put the beaten egg on another and the breadcrumbs on a third plate. Coat the fish in the seasoned flour, then in beaten egg, then breadcrumbs to coat completely.

- Place the fish on a piece of baking parchment on a separate baking sheet. Bake the fish on the centre shelf and the chips on the top shelf for 15 minutes, then swap the positions so the chips are in centre, and the fish on top. Move and turn the chips for even browning and cook a further 10–15 minutes until both are golden and cooked through.

Cook's tip: You don't have to use potatoes for chips! Try celeriac, sweet potato, pumpkin or parsnips for delectable results and to make them part of your five a day then (potatoes don't count as they are considered as carbohydrates, not vegetables for vitamins and minerals!).

• From the Chippy

Makes 4 large cakes

Quick Fish Cakes

Preparation time:
10 minutes

Cooking time:
6 minutes

To freeze:
Pack in a rigid container, interleaved with baking parchment if necessary, and freeze for up to 2 months

These traditionally used cooked leftover fish from the chippie to stop it being wasted and you can use 200g cooked white fish (or mixed white and smoked fish) instead of the drained can of salmon. You can serve them with chips and peas but I prefer a green salad.

- If you are cooking the potatoes, prick with a fork and microwave for about 6 minutes until they feel tender when squeezed. Leave to cool, then peel. Alternatively, peel, cut in small chunks and boil for 10–15 minutes until tender, then drain.

- Put the potato in a bowl and add the fish. Mash together thoroughly, then add the lemon juice, chilli powder, capers and seasoning to taste. Moisten with the milk and add a little of the beaten egg to bind. Shape the mixture into 4 flat cakes.

- Dip the cakes in the remaining egg, then in the breadcrumbs to coat completely.

- Heat the oil in a frying pan and fry the cakes for about 3 minutes each side until crisp and golden brown. Drain on kitchen paper.

- Serve hot with a wedge of lemon to squeeze over.

2 potatoes (or 350g cooked potato)
185g can tuna, drained
2 spring onions, finely chopped
2 tsp lemon juice
Good pinch of chilli powder
1 tbsp pickled capers, chopped
Salt and freshly ground black pepper
2 tbsp milk
1 egg, beaten
50g natural dried breadcrumbs
Sunflower oil for frying

To serve
Lemon wedges

Preparation time:
10 minutes
Cooking time:
10–15 minutes
To freeze:
Best eaten fresh

Serves 4

Pig in a Crispy Blanket

A little sunflower oil
8 extra-lean pork sausages
2 sheets of filo pastry
A little tomato ketchup

To serve
Baked beans or Mushy Peas
(page 85) and Easy
Pickled Eggs (page 86)

For a traditional battered sausage you can dip sausages in seasoned flour then in the batter on page 80 and deep-fry for about 6 minutes until cooked through – but they're lethal calorie-wise! So I've come up with a delicious (and more sophisticated) solution!

- Brush a frying pan lightly with sunflower oil, heat the pan, then brown the sausages quickly all over. Remove from the pan and leave to cool.

- Preheat the oven to 200°C/gas 6.

- Brush each sheet of filo with a little sunflower oil and fold in half widthways. Spread each with a little tomato ketchup, then cut in 4 equal long strips. Starting at one point of a strip, place a sausage diagonally on the pastry, then roll up so the pastry overlaps in a spiral round the sausage, leaving just the tip of the sausage showing. Place on a baking sheet. Repeat with the remaining sausages and pastry strips. Brush again lightly with oil.

- Bake in the oven for 15–20 minutes until crisp and golden and the sausages are cooked through.

- Serve hot with baked beans or mushy peas and pickled eggs.

• From the Chippy

Serves 4

Mushy Peas

Preparation time:
5 minutes
Cooking time:
10 minutes
To freeze:
Pack in a rigid container, seal
and freeze for up to 6 months

These are traditionally made with dried marrowfat peas and need long soaking before cooking. My version uses frozen garden ones; it tastes great and is far, far quicker to make. It's perfect with any of the pies in the pie shop section too.

Large knob of butter
225g frozen peas
4 tbsp milk
½ tsp dried mint
Salt and freshly ground black
  pepper

- Melt the butter in a saucepan.

- Add the peas, milk, mint and a little salt and pepper. Bring to the boil, stirring, reduce the heat, cover and simmer very gently for 10 minutes until really soft.

- Crush the peas with a potato masher to break them up into the liquid so you end up with a thick, lumpy 'mush'.

Preparation time:
5 minutes plus cooling
Cooking time:
6 minutes
To freeze:
Not suitable for freezing

Serves 4

Easy Pickled Eggs

4 eggs
About 175ml white vinegar
½ tsp caster sugar
Pinch of salt
6 peppercorns
1 bay leaf

There is often a huge jar of these sitting on the counter in traditional fish and chip shops. You can make a whole jarful of these and store them in the fridge for several weeks if you're in the mood or have a load of eggs.

- Put the eggs in a small saucepan and just cover with cold water. Bring to the boil, then boil for 6 minutes.

- Drain and plunge immediately into cold water. When cool, remove the shells.

- Meanwhile, bring the vinegar, sugar, salt and bay leaf to the boil in a separate pan. Remove from the heat.

- Pack the eggs in a small container (either a clean glass jar or plastic container with a sealable lid) that will hold them tightly. Pour the hot, not boiling, vinegar, including the peppercorns, over the top. Tuck the bay leaf in the container too. Top up with extra vinegar if necessary. Cover and leave to cool.

- Ideally, chill in the fridge for several days before use but they can be eaten immediately they are cold.

• From the Chippy

Serves 4

Preparation time:
5 minutes
To freeze:
Not suitable for freezing

Quick Tartare Sauce

This is a quick version of the classic sauce that goes so well with almost any fish, but is perfect with fish and chips. If you have the capers and/or olives in your fridge, they are really good to use but you can just use the cucumber if not.

> **Speed tip:** You don't have to make your own – you can buy a good-quality jar and add a little dried thyme or dill to enhance the flavour. Store the remainder in the fridge – it keeps for ages!

5cm piece cucumber, peeled
2 tsp pickled capers, chopped
4 stoned, green olives, chopped
4 tbsp mayonnaise
2 tsp vinegar from the caper jar
½ tsp dried dill or thyme
Pinch of caster sugar
1 tbsp chopped fresh parsley (optional)

- Finely dice the cucumber. Squeeze out any excess moisture and place in a small bowl.

- Add the remaining ingredients and mix well.

- Cover and chill for several hours to allow the flavours to develop, if you have time, before serving.

From the Burger Joint

Home-made burgers are a great, big, hearty meal enjoyed by all the family. Here I've created my own version of the original hamburger plus some exciting other burgers for you to try. I've even come up with a way to make those moreish thin fries. They are a bit fiddly but delectable! There are plenty of cheat ideas too and all of them have accompaniments to turn them into nutritious, balanced meals. Oh, another tip, if you have children, they may not be able to eat quite such whoppers, so simply shape the burgers as for the double cheeseburgers but allow just one patty per child. You don't have to have fries, either. Try the delicious Jacket-baked Potatoes with Soured Cream and Chives recipe on page 110, or the Golden Oven Wedges on page 111 for a delicious change.

Takeaway Tip

Mini-burgers: Look out for little soft dinner rolls, which make great mini-burger buns for little appetites or for snack meals. You can simply shape smaller burgers to fit the size of the rolls. The cooking time won't change as the thickness will be the same.

CHAPTER 7

Preparation time:
5 minutes

Cooking time:
6–8 minutes

To freeze:
Only freeze if fresh, not frozen, mince was used; freeze raw, interleaved with clingfilm in a rigid container for up to 3 months

450g lean minced steak
1 small onion, grated (or
    1 tsp onion granules or
    2 tsp onion purée)
Salt and freshly ground black
    pepper
1 small egg, beaten
3–4 tbsp plain flour
1 tbsp sunflower oil
4 burger buns, split
A little tomato ketchup
A little mild American or
    French mustard
A few slices of dill pickled
    cucumber
2 tomatoes, thinly sliced
Large handful of shredded
    crisp lettuce

To serve
Matchstick French Fries
    (page 96) and a large
    mixed salad

Serves 4

Classic Hamburgers with All the Trimmings

Choose good-quality extra-lean mince. Cheaper minced beef contains a lot of fat and your burgers will shrink drastically and be greasy. Lean meat ones shrink too unless you add the egg (or milk) and the hole-making in the middle also works!

- Put the meat and onion in a bowl and season well, working the flavour into the meat with your hands. Work in enough egg to bind the mixture, but take care not to make it too wet (keep any remainder in the fridge to glaze pastry or make more hamburgers to freeze).

- With well-floured hands, divide the meat in quarters and shape each into a patty 10–12 cm in diameter (depending on the size of your burger buns). Press it together to flatten firmly. Press your forefinger through the centre to make a small hole (it will close as it cooks). Chill for 30 minutes, if possible.

- Either brush the burgers with oil and cook under a hot preheated grill, or heat the sunflower oil in a non-stick frying pan and fry the burgers for 3 minutes each side until browned on the outside and cooked to your liking. Drain on kitchen paper.

- Spread the insides of the buns with ketchup and mustard and put the bun bases on plates. Top with the burgers, then the sliced dill picked cucumber, tomato slices and shredded lettuce, and finally the top of the buns.

- Serve with the matchstick French fries and a fresh salad.

• From the Burger Joint

Serves 4

Double Cheese Burgers

Preparation time:
15 minutes
Cooking time:
8–12 minutes
To freeze:
Only freeze if fresh, not frozen, mince was used. Freeze raw, interleaved with clingfilm in a rigid container for up to 3 months

This is a mighty meal and, ideally, is good using ready-sliced cheese that is uniform in shape and thickness. Fast food chains use processed cheese, but easy-melt Swiss cheese is better. You could use sliced Cheddar if you prefer.

- Put the meat and onion in a bowl, season well and add the mixed herbs. Work the flavourings well into the meat with your hands. Work in the milk. Divide the mixture into 8 equal pieces. Shape each piece into a patty about 10–12 cm diameter (depending on the size of your burger buns) and place on a board. Flatten firmly with the palm of your hand. Make a small hole in the centre of each with your finger. Chill for 30 minutes, if possible.

- Brush with the oil and grill under a hot preheated grill or fry, 4 at a time, in a non-stick frying pan for 2 minutes each side until browned and cooked to your liking. Keep warm whilst cooking the remainder.

- Spread the inside of the buns with ketchup and English mustard, and put the bases of the buns on plates. Top each with a burger then slice of cheese, then some onion, dill pickles, tomato and rocket or lettuce. Repeat the layers then cover with the bun tops. Press down firmly with your hand and serve with matchstick French fries and extra salad.

450g lean minced steak
1 small onion, grated (or
   1 tsp onion granules or
   2 tsp onion purée)
Salt and freshly ground black
   pepper
1 tsp dried mixed herbs
1 tbsp milk
2 tbsp sunflower oil
4 burger buns
Tomato ketchup
Mild American or French
   mustard
8 thin slices Emmental or
   Leerdammer cheese
1 small onion, very finely
   chopped
A few dill picked cucumber
   slices
2 tomatoes, thinly sliced
Handful of rocket or
   shredded crisp lettuce

To serve
Matchstick French Fries
   (page 96) and extra salad

Preparation time:
19 minutes
Cooking time:
6–8 minutes
To freeze:
Only freeze if fresh, not frozen, mince was used; freeze raw, interleaved with clingfilm in a rigid container for up to 3 months

350g minced chicken
1 onion, grated (or 1 tsp onion granules or 2 tsp onion purée)
1 garlic clove, crushed (or ½ tsp garlic purée)
2 Weetabix (or 2 handfuls of white breadcrumbs)
1 tsp dried thyme
Salt and freshly ground black pepper
1 small egg, beaten
A little plain flour, for dusting
1 tbsp sunflower oil
4 rashers smoked back bacon
4 English muffins, split, and toasted on the cut sides
Handful of shredded crisp lettuce
1 ripe avocado, mashed with a dash of lemon juice (optional)
2 tbsp redcurrant jelly
2 tbsp mayonnaise

To serve
Root Crisps (page 97) and extra salad

Serves 4

Chicken and Bacon Burgers

You can, of course, omit the bacon and just have a simple chicken burger or add a slice of ham instead of the bacon. I like spreading the burger bun with the redcurrant jelly (or you could use cranberry sauce) but you can stick to ketchup if you prefer.

• Put the chicken in a bowl and add the grated onion. Crumble in the Weetabix and add the thyme and some salt and pepper. Mix thoroughly with the hands and then mix in the beaten egg to bind.

• With floured hands, divide the mixture in quarters and shape into 4 patties about 10cm in diameter. Place on a board and flatten with the palm of the hand. Chill for 30 minutes, if possible.

• Heat the oil in a non-stick frying pan. Fry the bacon on both sides until browned and cooked through. Drain on kitchen paper. Wrap in foil and keep warm.

• Re-heat the pan and fry the burgers over a moderate heat for 3–4 minutes on each side until golden and cooked through. Drain on kitchen paper.

• Place the bases of the muffins on plates. Top with the burgers, then the bacon, then the avocado, if using, then some shredded lettuce.

• Spread the toasted side of the muffin tops with redcurrant jelly then mayonnaise. Place on top of the lettuce. Press down firmly and serve with vegetable crisps and extra salad.

• From the Burger Joint

Serves 4

Sausage Burgers with Mushrooms and Apple

Preparation time:
5 minutes
Cooking time:
10–12 minutes
To freeze:
Only freeze if fresh, not frozen, sausagemeat was used; freeze raw, interleaved with clingfilm in a rigid container for up to 3 months

Choose good-quality sausagemeat for the best flavour and texture (some have far too much fat). You can make pork burgers like the chicken ones on page 92, using minced pork, flavoured with sage instead of thyme, and serve them in the same way as this burger.

450g pork sausagemeat
1 tsp dried sage
Freshly ground black pepper
4 large portabello mushrooms
1 tbsp sunflower oil
4 burger buns, split
Dijon or grainy mustard
3–4 tbsp apple sauce (home-cooked or from a jar) or apple chutney
2 tbsp mayonnaise

To serve
Large mixed salad

Speed tip: Grill and halve sausages and serve like burgers with the mushrooms and the apple topping

- Preheat the grill.

- Put the sausagemeat in a bowl, add the sage and some pepper and work in with the hands. With wetted hands, shape the mixture into 4 patties about 10–12 cm in diameter (depending on the size of your burger buns). Flatten slightly.

- Trim the stalks from the mushrooms and peel them if the skins feel tough when a little is pulled off. Brush all over with the oil and season them with pepper.

- Grill the burgers under a moderate grill for 5–6 minutes each side until browned and cooked through. Half way through cooking, add the mushrooms gill-sides up.

- Spread the cut side of the base of the buns with a little Dijon or grainy mustard, then top with the mushrooms, then the burgers, then apple sauce or chutney. Spread the mayonnaise over the cut sides of the tops of the buns, place on top of the burgers and press down gently.

- Serve with a generous salad.

Veggie Burgers

Preparation time:
10 minutes
Cooking time:
6–8 minutes
To freeze:
Best frozen raw; wrap each burger in clingfilm and freeze in a rigid container for up to 3 months

425g can of red kidney
   beans, drained
2 carrots, grated
1 small onion, grated (or
   1 tsp onion granules or
   2 tsp onion purée)
25g chopped mixed nuts
1 Weetabix or a handful of
   fresh breadcrumbs
1 tsp dried mixed herbs
1 tbsp Worcestershire sauce
Salt and freshly ground black
   pepper
1 small egg, beaten
Sunflower oil
4 burger buns, toasted on
   cut sides
2 tomatoes, sliced
A few thin slices cucumber
Tomato ketchup or sweet
   chilli sauce

To serve
Matchstick French Fries
   (page 96) or Chips (page
   80), Coleslaw (page 106)
   and a green salad

Any can of beans or lentils can be used for this burger. Make sure you use vegetarian Worcestershire sauce if this is being served to true vegetarians. Spice up the mixture with a few drops of Tabasco, if liked.

Speed tip: Use low-fat oven chips and bought coleslaw instead of making your own

- Mash the beans well in a bowl with a potato masher or fork. Add the carrots, onion, nuts, Weetabix or breadcrumbs, Worcestershire sauce and some salt and pepper. Mix well, then mix with enough of the beaten egg to bind the mixture together. Don't make it too wet.

- Shape the mixture into 4 burgers and chill for 30 minutes to firm up.

- Heat enough oil to cover the base of a large non-stick frying pan. Fry the burgers over a moderate heat for 3–4 minutes on each side until golden brown. Drain on kitchen paper.

- Place the burgers on the bases of the buns. Top with some sliced tomatoes and cucumber. Spread the cut sides of the bun tops with ketchup or sweet chilli sauce, place on top and press down.

- Serve with fries or chips, coleslaw and a green salad.

• From the Burger Joint

Serves 4

Fish Fillet Burgers

Preparation time:
10 minutes
Cooking time:
6 minutes
To freeze:
Only freeze if fresh, not frozen,
fish was used; open-freeze the
coated fish raw, then store in a
sealable freezer bag for up to
3 months

A delicious treat for all the family for lunch or supper. Try using
salmon instead of white fish and topping with home-made Coleslaw
(page 106) or good-quality bought slaw instead of the tartare sauce.
I like to add celery salt instead of ordinary salt to the crumbs, too.

> **Speed tip:** Use 3–4 good-quality pure fillet fish fingers per
> person instead of crumbing your own pieces of fish and serve
> with low-fat oven French fries.

- Preheat the grill.

- Wipe the fish well to dry it. Mix the flour with a little salt and
  pepper on a plate. Beat the egg on a separate plate. Put the
  crumbs on another and season well with salt, pepper and the
  paprika.

- Dip the fish in the flour to coat, then in the egg, draining off
  excess, then the crumbs to coat completely.

- Heat about 5mm sunflower oil in a non-stick frying pan. Fry the
  fish for about 3 minutes each side until crisp, golden and cooked
  through.

- Put the bun bases on plates. Top with a few pickled cucumber
  slices and some shredded lettuce, then the fish. Spoon the tartare
  sauce on top, then cover with the bun lids.

- Serve with fries and green beans.

4 small chunky portions of
coley or sustainable cod,
cut from the thick end of
the fillet and skinned,
about 90g each (or frozen
block portions, just
thawed)
2 tbsp plain flour
1 egg
50g natural dried
breadcrumbs
Salt and freshly ground black
pepper
1 tsp sweet paprika
Sunflower oil
4 burger buns, split
A few fresh or dill pickled
cucumber slices
2 large handfuls of shredded
lettuce
4 tbsp tartare sauce

To serve
Matchstick French Fries
(page 96) and green beans

Matchstick French Fries

Preparation time:
15 minutes (including initial cooking) plus chilling

Cooking time:
6–8 minutes

To freeze:
After the initial 1 minute fry and cool (or tossing in oil), spread out on a baking sheet and open-freeze until firm, then pack in sealable freezer bags and store in the freezer for up to 4 months

4 large fairly floury potatoes
A few ice cubes
2 tbsp lemon juice
Sunflower oil
Salt

Making perfect thin fries is not that simple. This works really well but takes a bit of effort. If you can't be bothered to do the first frying, toss the hot, boiled, dried chips in a little sunflower oil to coat, then chill, if time, or freeze before you fry.

Speed tip: Use low-fat frozen oven French fries instead!

- Peel the potatoes and cut into 5mm matchsticks. Place immediately in a bowl of cold water with the ice cubes added.

- Bring a pan of water to the boil with the lemon juice added. Drain the fries and add to the pan. Bring back to the boil and boil for 3 minutes. Drain well, then dry the fries in a clean cloth.

- Heat 1cm sunflower oil in a large pan until a chip dropped in rises to the surfaces sizzling furiously (or to 190°C in a deep-fat fryer). Fry the chips for 1 minute only. Remove with a slotted spoon and drain thoroughly on kitchen paper.

- Leave to cool then chill for at least 30 minutes (or freeze to cook another day).

- Reheat the oil to 190°C again and fry the fries in two batches for 3–4 minutes until crisp and golden. Keep warm in a low oven whilst you cook the remainder. Sprinkle with a little salt – but not too much!

- From the Burger Joint

Serves 4

Root Crisps

Preparation time:
15 minutes
Cooking time:
10–24 minutes
To freeze:
Not suitable for freezing; store
any unused crisps in an airtight
container

These are great with burgers, grilled meat, chicken or fish – or as a healthy snack. You can fry them in hot oil for about 2 minutes, in small batches, then drain well on kitchen paper – but that's not as good for you! Cook just one or two types of vegetable if you prefer.

½ sweet potato, peeled
1 beetroot, peeled
1 small parsnip, peeled
1 large carrot, peeled
Sunflower oil

- Use a potato peeler, slicer on your grater, the thin slicing blade for a food processor, or a mandolin to very thinly slice all the vegetables.

- Lay the vegetable slices in a single layer on several large microwave-safe dinner plates. Microwave each plateful for about 3 minutes until each slice is shrivelled to half the size and dry but still brightly coloured.

- Tip onto a cold plate to cool and crisp up. Repeat with the other plates. If, once cold, they are still not quite crisp, microwave for another 20–30 seconds.

- Alternatively, spread out in a single layer on non-stick baking sheets and bake in a preheated oven at 200°C/gas 6 for about 10 minutes. Again, they'll crisp as they cool but if they don't feel completely dry, turn off the oven and leave to cool inside.

From the Chicken Shack

Okay, this isn't KFC and I don't pretend to have infiltrated his secret recipe but these make really tasty, crunchy chicken pieces that will tickle the taste buds. Frying chicken in a pan is a tricky business to get right so I've oven-baked these for perfect results every time. There are nuggets (with a great barbecue dipping sauce, of course) and sticky wings, too, both particularly popular with younger members of the family.

You'll find all the accompaniments you need, as well, from barbecued beans to coleslaw and delicious potato wedges, fluffy mash and roasted corn cobs. I've even included a delicious chicken wrap for a quick TV supper (or good cold in the lunchbox for a treat, too), and fluffy mash – the perfect alternative accompaniment.

Takeaway Tip

Savoury coating: For a delicious crunchy coating, use a packet of dry stuffing mix – such as sage and onion or parsley, thyme and lemon – instead of the crumb mixtures suggested in the recipes.

CHAPTER 8

Preparation time:
10 minutes

Cooking time:
45 minutes

To freeze:
Only freeze if using fresh (not thawed, frozen) chicken; freeze coated but raw in a rigid container for up to 6 months

Sunflower oil
100ml milk
4 tbsp plain (all-purpose) flour
Salt and freshly ground black pepper
75g natural dried breadcrumbs
2 tsp dried thyme
4 chicken leg portions, cut in 2 at the joint (or 4 chicken drumsticks and 4 chicken thighs), skinned

To garnish
Watercress and cucumber

To serve
Golden Oven Wedges (page 111) and Coleslaw (page 106)

Oven-fried Chicken

The chicken can be coated and chilled in the fridge for several hours or overnight before cooking if more convenient (obviously, don't preheat the oven until you are ready to cook it them though!). Experiment with different herbs in the coating, too.

- Preheat the oven to 200°C/gas 6. Pour in enough sunflower oil to cover the base of a roasting tin and place it in the oven to heat.

- Put the milk in a shallow dish. Mix the flour and a little salt and pepper in a separate shallow dish and the dried crumbs and the thyme in a third dish.

- Dip the chicken in the milk, then the flour mixture, then the milk again, then the crumbs to coat completely.

- Place the chicken in the hot oil. Tilt the tin and baste the chicken with the oil. Bake for about 45 minutes until golden and cooked through.

- Drain on kitchen paper, place on plates, garnish with plenty of watercress and cucumber and serve with oven wedges and coleslaw.

• From the Chicken Shack

Serves 4

Savoury-coated Crispy Fried Chicken

Preparation time:
10 minutes plus chilling
Cooking time:
45 minutes
To freeze:
Only if using fresh (not thawed, frozen) chicken; freeze coated but raw in a rigid container for up to 6 months

The semolina or polenta adds extra crunch to the savoury coating in this recipe, but you can use all breadcrumbs, if you prefer. You can, of course, substitute chicken breast fillets, cut in halves, instead of the legs and thighs.

- Mix the breadcrumbs with the semolina or polenta, onion, salt and spices in a shallow dish. Put the flour in a separate dish and beat the egg in a third.

- Dip the chicken in the flour, then the beaten egg, draining well, then the breadcrumbs to coat completely. Chill for 30 minutes, if possible.

- Preheat the oven to 200°C/gas 6. Heat enough oil to just cover the base of a baking tin.

- Lay the chicken in the tin and carefully turn over in the oil or tilt the tin and baste the chicken with the hot oil. Cook for 45 minutes until crisp and golden. Drain on kitchen paper.

- Transfer to plates, garnish with lime wedges and serve with barbecued baked beans, fluffy mashed potatoes and a mixed salad.

60g natural dried breadcrumbs
25g semolina or polenta
1 small onion, grated (or 1 tsp onion granules or 2 tsp onion purée)
½ tsp salt
1 tbsp Cajun spices
2 tbsp plain flour
1 egg
4 leg chicken portions, cut in 2 at the joint (or 4 chicken drumsticks and 4 thighs), skinned (optional)
Sunflower oil

To garnish
Lime wedges

To serve
Barbecued Beans (page 108), Fluffy Mash (page 107) and a mixed salad

Preparation time:
10 minutes
Cooking time:
45 minutes
To freeze:
Pack in a sealable freezer bag and freeze for up to 2 months; thaw, then reheat in the microwave or a moderate oven, or serve cold

1 garlic clove, crushed
  (or ½ tsp garlic purée)
1 tbsp clear honey
½ tsp English mustard
4 tbsp tomato ketchup
2 tbsp tomato purée
1 tbsp Worcestershire sauce
1 tbsp soy sauce
2 tsp smoked paprika
12 chicken wings (about
  900g)

To serve
Jacket Potatoes with Soured Cream and Chives (page 110), Roasted Corn Cobs (page 109) and a large mixed salad

Serves 4

Smoky Glazed Chicken Wings

Everybody's favourite finger food! Buy the small wings, not the whole wing portion including the breasts. You can vary the flavour by adding half five-spice powder and half sweet paprika instead of the smoked paprika and omitting the Worcestershire sauce.

- Preheat the oven to 200°C/gas 6.

- Cut off the wing tips at the first joint with scissors and discard or use to make stock.

- Mix all the ingredients except the chicken in a large bowl. Add the chicken and toss until evenly coated.

- Line a large roasting tin with baking parchment (to prevent the mixture burning onto the tin). Add the chicken in a single layer.

- Roast in the oven for about 40 minutes, turning once, until cooked through and glazed.

- Pile onto a serving platter and serve with jacket-baked potatoes with soured cream and chives, roasted corn cobs and a large mixed salad. They are also good served cold.

• From the Chicken Shack

Serves 4

Chicken Nuggets with Barbecue Dipping Sauce

Preparation time:
15 minutes plus chilling
Cooking time:
6 or 12 minutes
To freeze:
Only if using fresh (not thawed frozen) chicken; arrange in a single layer on a baking sheet and open-freeze until firm, then pack in a sealable freezer bag and freeze for up to 6 months

These tasty morsels have a lovely cereal coating which makes them extra-crunchy. You can buy matzo meal in all good supermarkets but you can, of course, use ordinary natural dried breadcrumbs if you prefer.

Speed tip: Buy bottled barbecue sauce instead of making your own – there's loads of choice.

- Toss the pieces of chicken in the flour.

- Mix the matzo meal with the remaining ingredients except the milk and oil.

- Dip the chicken in the milk and then roll in the matzo meal mixture. Repeat the dipping and coating. Chill for 30 minutes, if you have time.

- Heat about 5mm sunflower oil in a deep frying pan until a few crumbs of matzo meal rise to the surface and sizzle immediately. Cook the nuggets in two batches, if necessary, turning once or twice and reheating the oil between batches, until crisp, golden and cooked through, about 6 minutes. Drain on kitchen paper.

- Meanwhile, mix the sauce ingredients together and spoon into small pots for dipping.

- Serve the nuggets with the dipping sauce, matchstick French fries, coleslaw and green beans.

For the chicken
4 skinless chicken breasts, cut into bite-sized chunks
4 tbsp plain flour
100g coarse matzo meal
1 tsp onion or garlic granules
½ tsp celery salt (or ordinary salt)
Freshly ground black pepper
2 tsp sweet paprika
4 tbsp milk
Sunflower oil

For the barbecue sauce
3 tbsp clear honey
3 tbsp tomato purée
1 tsp smoked paprika (optional)
2 tbsp soy sauce
1 tbsp Worcestershire sauce
1 tbsp red wine vinegar

To serve
Matchstick French Fries (page 96), Coleslaw (page 106) and French beans

Preparation time:
10 minutes plus marinating

Cooking time:
12 minutes

To freeze:
The cooked chicken can be frozen in a sealable freezer bag for up to 2 months

Serves 4

Chilli Chicken Salad Wrap

2 tbsp sunflower oil, plus extra for brushing
1 tbsp tomato ketchup
1 tbsp soy sauce
2 tsp Cajun spices
1/4 tsp chilli powder
4 small skinless chicken breasts
4 large flour tortillas (Mediterranean wraps)
4 tbsp mayonnaise
4 tbsp tomato salsa from a jar
4 small handfuls of shredded lettuce
1/4 cucumber, cut into matchsticks
4 cherry tomatoes, sliced

You can use the Chicken Nuggets (page 103) for putting in the wrap, if you like, just cut the chicken in strips rather than chunks before cooking. The griddled chicken is also delicious served on top of a Caesar salad (which you can buy in bags in supermarkets).

- Mix 1 tbsp of the sunflower oil with the ketchup, soy sauce and spices in a shallow dish. Make several slashes in the chicken and place in the marinade. Turn to coat completely. Cover and chill for several hours or overnight, if possible.

- Heat a griddle pan or the grill. Griddle or grill the chicken for about 6 minutes each side until golden and cooked through, turning once and brushing with a little more oil before and after turning.

- Transfer to a board and cut into thick, diagonal slices.

- Spread the tortillas with a little mayonnaise and salsa, leaving a border all round. Add some lettuce, cucumber, the tomatoes and the chicken. Fold the bottom and sides of the tortilla over the food, then roll up firmly to form a wrap. Cut each in half for serving.

• From the Chicken Shack

Crispy Fillet Burger with Pepper Mayonnaise

Preparation time:
10 minutes
Cooking time:
8 minutes
To freeze:
Best eaten fresh

This burger actually can be fried easily without worrying that you are going to burn the outside and leave the inside raw! It has a similar taste and texture to that famous recipe! It's sure to be a great family favourite.

For the mayonnaise
4 tbsp mayonnaise
1 tsp grainy mustard
1 tsp coarse ground black
  pepper

- Mix the mayonnaise with the grainy mustard and pepper. Chill until ready to serve.

For the chicken
4 skinless chicken breasts
6 tbsp plain flour
1 egg, beaten
2 tbsp Cajun spice blend
2 tsp dried thyme
Freshly ground black pepper
Sunflower oil for frying
4 torpedo buns
Crisp lettuce

- Put each fillet in a plastic bag and beat with a meat mallet or rolling pin to flatten slightly.

- Put 2 tbsp of the flour on one plate, the beaten egg on a second plate and the remaining flour mixed with the spices and herbs on a third plate.

- Dip the chicken in the flour, then the beaten egg, then the spice mix to coat completely.

- Heat about 5mm oil in a large frying pan until a cube of day-old bread browns in 30 seconds. Add the chicken, turn down the heat and fry gently for 4 minutes each side until crisp, golden and cooked through. Drain on kitchen paper.

- Split the rolls, add some crispy lettuce, top with the chicken, then some pepper mayonnaise and eat straight away.

Preparation time:
5–15 minutes (depending on whether you have a machine or are shredding by hand) plus chilling
To freeze:
Not suitable for freezing

Serves 4

Coleslaw

1 small white cabbage (about 450g)
2 large carrots, coarsely grated
1 small onion, grated
8 tbsp mayonnaise
2 tbsp sunflower oil
2 tbsp white wine vinegar
1 tsp caster sugar
½ tsp English (or Dijon) mustard
Salt and freshly ground black pepper

This is so simple and inexpensive to make at home and something that can keep in the fridge for several days so it's worth making a tub full! If you have a food processor, it makes light work of the veggie shredding.

- Finely shred the cabbage, discarding the thick central stump. Place in a bowl with the carrots and onion.

- Mix the mayonnaise with the oil, vinegar and flavourings. Add to the vegetables and toss thoroughly. Place in a container with a sealable lid and chill for at least 30 minutes to allow the flavours to develop.

• From the Chicken Shack

Serves 4

Fluffy Mash

Preparation time:
10 minutes
Cooking time:
15 minutes
To freeze:
Spoon into a rigid container and
freeze for up to 3 months

It's important to use fairly floury potatoes, like King Edwards, to get good mash with no lumps. As a delicious variation, add 75g grated strong Cheddar cheese to the hot mash and beat well until melted. Alternatively, use half celeriac and half potato.

- Cut the potatoes into small chunks. Boil in lightly salted water for about 15 minutes until really tender.

- Drain thoroughly and return to the pan. Mash thoroughly with the milk and butter, then season to taste and beat well until fluffy.

- For a touch of decadence, serve spooned onto plates, with a small dip in the top. Add a tiny knob of butter to each so it melts into a pool.

1kg fairly floury potatoes,
    peeled
Salt and freshly ground black
    pepper
4 tbsp milk
Good knob of butter, plus
    extra to garnish

Preparation time:
5 minutes
Cooking time:
8–10 minutes
To freeze:
Freeze in a rigid container for up
to 6 months

Serves 4

Barbecued Beans

150ml passata
1 small grated onion (or
   1 tsp onion granules or
   2 tsp onion purée)
1 tsp smoked paprika
1 tbsp clear honey
1 tbsp Worcestershire sauce
1 large can of haricot beans,
   drained and rinsed

Delicious-tasting beans bathed in a lightly spiced, barbecue and tomato sauce go really well with any of the fried or baked chicken dishes but are also delicious with sausages or eggs for a quick, tasty supper.

Speed tip: Use ready-made baked beans and stir in a little bottled barbecue sauce, or just some smoked paprika and a splash of brown sauce

- Mix the passata with the onion, paprika, honey and Worcestershire sauce in a small saucepan.

- Add the beans, stir well, bring to the boil, then reduce the heat and simmer gently for 8–10 minutes until the beans are bathed in a rich sauce, stirring occasionally.

• From the Chicken Shack

Serves 4

Roasted Corn Cobs

Preparation time:
5 minutes
Cooking time:
25–30 minutes
To freeze:
Not suitable for freezing

When corn is in season, roast it whole in the husks, with just the silks pulled off, then melt the butter with the thyme and pour it over after you peel off the husks. Try this on the barbecue in summer too.

50g butter, softened
1 tsp dried thyme
4 whole or 8 halves of
    prepared corn cobs,
    thawed if frozen
Salt and freshly ground black
    pepper

- Preheat the oven to 200°C/gas 6.

- Cut 4 squares of foil large enough to wrap 1 whole or 2 halves of corn. Smear the centres of each with a quarter of the butter. Sprinkle with the thyme. Place the corn on the butter and sprinkle with a little salt and pepper. Wrap tightly to make sure the butter doesn't leak out.

- Place on a baking sheet with the fold of foil on top. Roast for 25–30 minutes until the corn is tender.

- Unwrap and serve with the buttery juices poured over.

Preparation time:
5 minutes
Cooking time:
60 minutes
To freeze:
Not suitable for freezing

Serves 4

Jacket Potatoes with Soured Cream and Chives

4 large potatoes, scrubbed

For the topping
A small handful of fresh
  chives, snipped, or
  1 spring onion, finely
  chopped
150ml soured cream, crème
  fraîche or thick plain
  yoghurt
Freshly ground black pepper

For a delicious and unusual change, bake small sweet potatoes instead of ordinary potatoes (or two larger ones which are easier to find, then cut each in half for serving) and add a pinch of ground cumin to the topping.

Speed tip: Wrap each pricked potato in kitchen paper, arrange on the turntable and microwave on HIGH for 12–15 minutes or until soft, then crisp the skin under a hot grill

- Preheat the oven to 200°C/gas 6.

- Prick the potatoes all over with a fork and thread on metal skewers. Bake in the oven for about 1 hour until soft when squeezed.

- Meanwhile make the topping: mix the chives or spring onions with the soured cream, crème fraîche or yoghurt in a small bowl. Season well with pepper, then chill until ready to serve.

- Remove the potatoes from the oven and make a cross-cut in the top of each. Squeeze slightly with an oven-gloved hand to open the tops. Place on serving plates and spoon the topping over.

• From the Chicken Shack

Serves 4

Golden Oven Wedges

Preparation time:
5 minutes
Cooking time:
40 minutes
To freeze:
Not suitable for freezing

This technique is particularly good with sweet potato and celeriac as well as potato. You can also try it with pumpkin, swede, parsnips or even large beetroot too (but they'll need peeling before use). Experiment to see what you like best.

700g even-sized potatoes, scrubbed
3 tbsp sunflower oil
2 tbsp black onion, caraway or sesame seeds (optional)
Coarse sea salt

- Preheat the oven to 200°C/gas 6.

- Cut the potatoes in halves, then each half into 3 or 4 wedges. Place on a baking sheet. Toss in the oil, then sprinkle all over with the seeds, if using.

- Bake in the oven for about 40 minutes until crisp and golden on the outside and soft in the middle, turning once.

- Sprinkle with a little coarse sea salt and serve hot.

From the Pie Shop

I defy anyone to say they haven't enjoyed a hot pie at one time or another in their lives. Whether you're a fan of the Cornish pasty or prefer something a little more elegant like a steak and stilton pie. Yes, they do take a bit of preparation but the flavours and texture you get making your own are immeasurable. It's worth bothering to precook the meat, in most cases, as then you get good, rich, meltingly tender filling that's a joy to eat.

The good thing is the fillings can be made in advance, if that suits better, but most are quite quick as I've used mince or little pieces of chicken. For the only longer one – the Steak, Guiness and Stilton Pies – you can use a pressure cooker to speed things up or a slow cooker to slow things down!

The filling really needs to be cold before topping with pastry as it's much easier to handle. If the filling is hot the pastry goes soggy very quickly as the fat in it melts and it can collapse into the gravy. If time is short, go for one of the quick pies with no pre-cooking – like Giant Sausage Rolls or Cheese, Tomato and Pesto Pies.

Takeaway Tip

Leftover pies: If you've made a casserole and have some left over, you can make it go a long way if you turn it into individual pies following any of our meat pie methods in this chapter (throw in a few sliced mushrooms, diced cooked vegetables or frozen peas to pad it out further).

Preparation time:
25 minutes
Cooking time:
40 minutes
To freeze:
Cook, cool, then freeze in a rigid container; thaw before reheating.

Serves 4

Cornish Pasties

1 potato, peeled and finely
  diced
1 carrot, finely diced
1 turnip, finely diced
1 onion, finely diced
200g lean minced lamb
1 tsp dried mixed herbs
Salt and freshly ground black
  pepper
500g ready-made shortcrust
  pastry, thawed if frozen
Beaten egg, to glaze

To serve
Baked beans, broccoli or
  leafy greens

Traditionally, they are just potato, onion and the lamb but I've added some extra root vegetables for flavour and goodness. They are a great way to use up leftover cooked lamb, too: simply dice, discarding excess fat, and mix with the prepared vegetables.

• Preheat the oven to 200°C/gas 6 and lightly grease a baking sheet.

• Mix all the vegetables in a large bowl. Stir in the mince, herbs, a little salt and lots of pepper.

• Roll out the pastry and cut into four 20cm rounds, using a small plate as a guide. Divide the filling amongst the centres of the pastry rounds. Brush the edges with beaten egg. Doing each pasty in turn, add 2–3 tbsp water to the filling, draw up the edges of the pastry over the filling, meeting in the middle over the top. Pinch together, then crimp between finger and thumb to form an attractive rippled edge down the centre of each pasty.

• Carefully transfer to a prepared baking sheet. Brush with beaten egg to glaze. Bake in the oven for 20 minutes until browned, then cover loosely with foil and bake for a further 20 minutes until the filling is cooked through and the pastry is crisp and richly golden.

• Serve hot with baked beans and broccoli or leafy greens.

• From the Pie Shop

Serves 4

Lamb and Mint Pies with Leeks and Carrots

Preparation time:
25 minutes

Cooking time:
30 minutes

To freeze:
Open-freeze the uncooked pie, then wrap in sealable freezer bags and store in the freezer for up to 3 months

These pies are a delicious twist on the more usual lamb ones, with plenty of veggies included. Ring the changes with other vegetables of your choice, such as turnips or swede, or even diced courgettes or aubergine (then try adding oregano instead of mint).

1 small onion, sliced
500g lean minced lamb
2 leeks, thinly sliced
2 carrots, thinly sliced
450ml lamb or chicken stock
2 tbsp plain flour
2 tbsp water
1 tbsp mint sauce from a jar
Salt and freshly ground black pepper
2 x 320g sheets ready-rolled shortcrust pastry, thawed if frozen
Milk, single cream or beaten egg, to glaze

To serve
New potatoes and broccoli

- Put the onion and mince into a saucepan and fry, stirring, until the meat is no longer pink and all the grains are separate.

- Add the leeks and carrots and continue to cook, stirring, for 2 minutes until the leek softens.

- Add the stock, bring to the boil, then reduce the heat and simmer for 5 minutes until the vegetables are tender.

- Blend the flour with the water and stir into the mixture. Bring to the boil, stirring until thickened. Stir in the mint sauce. Season to taste. Set aside to cool.

- Preheat the oven to 200°C/gas 6.

- Cut out 4 'lids' of pastry, using the individual foil or porcelain pie dishes as a guide. Use the remaining pastry to line the pie dishes, patching and pressing together to fit. Spoon in the cool filling. Brush the edges of the pies with water and place the lids in position. Trim, then pinch together between finger and thumb all round. Transfer to a baking sheet. Brush the tops with milk, single cream or beaten egg to glaze. Make a small hole in the centre of each to allow steam to escape.

- Bake in the oven for about 30 minutes until golden and crisp on top. Serve hot with new potatoes and broccoli.

Preparation time:
15 minutes plus cooling
Cooking time:
20 minutes
To freeze:
Open-freeze the uncooked pies, then wrap in sealable freezer bags and store in the freezer for up to 3 months

Serves 4

Steak and Onion Pasties

2 onions, chopped (or
  2 large handfuls of
  frozen chopped onions)
1 carrot, coarsely grated
300g lean minced steak
2 tbsp plain flour
175ml beef stock
½ tsp dried thyme
2 tbsp soy sauce
Salt and freshly ground black
  pepper
375g ready-made shortcrust
  pastry, thawed if frozen
Milk, single cream or beaten
  egg, to glaze

To serve
Mustard, pickles and leafy
  greens

These pasties taste great with cauliflower cheese, which is quick to make. Just put cooked cauliflower in a dish and cover with some seasoned crème fraîche mixed with some grated Cheddar cheese and bake with the pies.

• Fry the onion and carrot with the minced steak, stirring until the meat is no longer pink and all the grains are separate.

• Stir in the flour and cook for 1 minute.

• Remove from the heat and stir in the stock, thyme, soy sauce, a little salt and lots of pepper. Return to the heat, bring to the boil, stirring, until thickened. Leave to cool.

• Preheat the oven to 200°C/gas 6 and grease a baking sheet.

• Roll out the pastry and cut into four 18 cm squares. Divide the filling between the centres of the squares. Brush the edges with water. Fold the pastry over the filling to form triangles. Press the edges together to seal and flute with the back of a knife.

• Transfer to the prepared baking sheet. Make a tiny hole in the top of each to allow steam to escape. Brush with milk, single cream or egg to glaze. Bake in the oven for about 20 minutes until crisp and golden brown.

• Serve hot with mustard, pickles and leafy greens.

Serves 4

Steak, Guinness and Stilton Pies

Preparation time:
2 hours (including cooking the meat) plus cooling
Cooking time:
20 minutes
To freeze:
Best freeze unbaked; open-freeze until firm, then wrap in sealable freezer bags and freeze for up to 3 months

If you can get skirt beef it's the best meat for these pies. Alternatively, lean braising steak is fine. Use bitter beer if you prefer it to Guinness, and other blue cheeses will do instead of Stilton (however, Danish Blue is a bit salty so go easy on the seasoning).

- Heat the oil in a saucepan. Add the onion and meat and fry for 3 minutes, stirring, until lightly golden.

- Add the mushrooms, stock, Guinness, soy sauce, a little seasoning and the bay leaf. Bring to the boil, then reduce the heat, cover and simmer very gently for 1½ hours until the beef is really tender.

- Blend the flour with the water and stir in to thicken the liquid. Simmer for 2 minutes. Transfer the meat mixture to 4 individual pie dishes. Crumble the Stilton over and stir in.

- Preheat the oven to 200°C/gas 6.

- Roll out the pastry. Cut a strip of pastry to go round the rim of each pie. Brush the pie dish rims with water and put the pastry in place. Brush with water. Cut four lids from the remaining pastry and place on top. Press the edges together to seal and flute with the back of a knife. Make a slit in the centre of each to allow steam to escape. Use the trimmings to decorate the pies, if liked. Transfer to a baking sheet.

- Brush the tops with milk, cream or beaten egg to glaze. Bake in the oven for about 20 minutes or until puffy and golden brown.

- Serve the pies with fluffy mash, peas and carrots.

1 tbsp sunflower oil
1 onion, chopped (or a large handful of frozen chopped onion)
700g skirt beef, cut into 1 cm dice
200g mushrooms, roughly chopped
300ml beef stock
330ml Guinness
1 tbsp soy sauce
Salt and freshly ground black pepper
1 bay leaf
3 tbsp plain flour
3 tbsp water
50g Stilton, crumbled
350g ready-made puff pastry, thawed if frozen

To serve
Fluffy Mash (page 107), peas and carrots

To pressure cook the filling:
After adding the Guinness and stock, pressure cook on HIGH pressure for 20 minutes, then reduce the pressure quickly under cold water
To slow cook the filling: Transfer to the slow cooker when boiling and slow cook for 6–8 hours

Preparation time:
45 minutes plus cooling time

Cooking time:
15–20 minutes

To freeze:
Best frozen unbaked; open-freeze until firm, then pack in sealable freezer bags and store in the freezer for up to 3 months

For the pies
700g lean minced steak
2 onions, chopped (or
    2 handfuls of frozen
    chopped onion)
150g mushrooms, sliced
1 large parsnip, cut into
    small dice
200ml brown ale
200ml beef stock
1 tbsp Worcestershire sauce
1 tsp tomato purée
1 bay leaf
Salt and freshly ground black
    pepper
3 tbsp plain flour
3 tbsp water
1 sheet ready-rolled puff
    pastry, thawed, if frozen
Beaten egg or a little single
    cream, to glaze

For the liquor
30g butter
2 tbsp cornflour
400ml chicken stock
2 tsp white wine vinegar
1 bouquet garni sachet
Handful of fresh parsley,
    chopped

To serve
Fluffy Mashed Potatoes
    (page 107), leafy greens
    and carrots

Serves 4

East End-style Pie and Liquor

This is based on a traditional London beef and ale pie recipe but there are numerous variations of this delicious, simple dish. I've added parsnips for extra flavour (and the veggie factor!). Substitute carrots, if you prefer.

- Put the beef and onions in a large saucepan. Fry, stirring, until the meat is no longer pink and all the grains are separate.

- Add the mushrooms, parsnip, beer, stock, Worcestershire sauce, tomato purée, bay leaf and some salt and pepper. Bring to the boil, then reduce the heat and simmer gently for 10 minutes until tender.

- Blend the flour and water together and stir into the pan. Bring back to the boil and cook, stirring, for 2 minutes.

- Taste and re-season, if necessary. Set aside to cool.

- Preheat the oven to 200°C/gas 6. Discard the bay leaf and spoon the mixture into 4 individual foil pie dishes.

- Cut the pastry into quarters. Trim a strip off each rectangle and lay round the rim of each pie dish. Brush with water, then place the pastry on top. Press all round to seal, then flute the edge with the back of a knife. Make a small slit in the centre to allow steam to escape. Place on a baking sheet. Brush the tops with beaten egg or single cream.

- Bake in the oven for about 20 minutes until puffy and golden brown.

• From the Pie Shop

- Meanwhile, make the liquor. Melt the butter in a small saucepan. Blend in the cornflour and cook, stirring, for 1 minute.

- Remove from the heat and gradually blend in the stock and add the vinegar and bouquet garni. Bring to the boil and simmer for 1 minute, stirring. Squeeze the bouquet garni against the side of the pan to extract maximum flavour then discard.

- Stir in the parsley and season to taste.

- Serve the pies with a little liquor spooned over accompanied by fluffy mashed potatoes, leafy greens and carrots.

Preparation time:
30 minutes plus cooling time

Cooking time:
20 minutes

To freeze:
Only freeze if you have used fresh (not cooked) chicken; open-freeze the uncooked pies until firm, then wrap in sealable freezer bags and freeze for up to 3 months

Good knob of butter
1 onion, finely chopped (or a large handful of frozen chopped onions)
6–8 boneless, skinless chicken thighs (or 4 small skinless chicken breasts), finely diced
100g button mushrooms, sliced
2 tbsp plain flour
200ml milk
1 tsp dried mixed herbs
Salt and freshly ground black pepper
2 tbsp single cream
100g frozen peas
375g ready-made shortcrust pastry, thawed if frozen
4 tsp redcurrant jelly (optional)
Milk or beaten egg, to glaze

To serve
New potatoes and green beans

Chicken and Mushroom Pies

You can make these with cooked leftover chicken if you have some. Simply make the mushroom sauce, stir in the chicken, then continue as in the recipe below. Add extra mushrooms or a drained can of sweetcorn if you haven't enough chicken.

Speed tip: Use a can of condensed mushroom soup with 2 tbsp single cream added instead of making your own sauce

- Melt the butter in a saucepan, add the onion and fry gently, stirring, for 3 minutes to soften.

- Add the chicken and mushrooms and fry a further 3 minutes, stirring.

- Stir in the flour and cook for 1 minute, stirring.

- Remove from the heat and gradually blend in the milk. Add the herbs. Return to the heat, bring to the boil and simmer for 2 minutes, stirring all the time.

- Season to taste and stir in the cream and peas. Set aside to cool.

- Preheat the oven to 200°C/gas 6 and grease a baking sheet.

- Roll out the pastry and cut into four 15 x 20 cm rectangles. Spoon the filling towards one end of the short ends of rectangle, leaving a border round the three sides and the other half of the rectangle clear. Brush the borders with water. Top the filling with a teaspoon of redcurrant jelly, if using.

• From the Pie Shop

- Fold the pastry over the filling and press the edges together to seal. Crimp all round the three sides between the finger and thumb. Carefully transfer the pies to the prepared baking sheet. Brush with milk or beaten egg to glaze. Bake in the oven for 20 minutes until crisp and golden.

- Serve hot with new potatoes and green beans.

Preparation time:
15 minutes
Cooking time:
30 minutes
To freeze:
Freeze cooked, or freeze raw
only if you used fresh, not
frozen, sausagemeat; open-
freeze until firm, then pack in
sealable freezer bags and freeze,
raw up to 2 months, cooked up
to 3 months

375g puff or shortcrust
    pastry, thawed if frozen
4 tbsp sweet pickle or
    tomato chutney
500g pure pork sausagemeat
Beaten egg, to glaze

To serve
Barbecued Beans (page 108)
    and a large mixed salad

Serves 4

Giant Sausage Rolls

If you make these yourself, you can ensure you buy top-quality
pure pork sausagemeat. Cheap ones contain far too much fat and
cereal and will not have the great, meaty flavour you desire. These
make a great cold snack lunch too with a few cherry tomatoes.

- Preheat the oven to 200°C/gas 6. Dampen a baking sheet, if you
  are using puff pastry, or lightly grease one, if using shortcrust.

- Roll out the pastry and cut into four 18cm squares.

- Spread the pickle down the centre of each pastry square. Divide
  the sausagemeat in quarters and, with wet hands, roll into sausage
  shapes about 18cm long. Lay them on top of the pickle.

- Brush the edges with beaten egg. Fold the pastry over the sausage
  and press the long edges well together to seal. Knock up and flute
  with the back of a knife. Make several slashes at intervals down
  the length of the rolls to decorate. Transfer to the prepared baking
  sheet and brush with beaten egg to glaze.

- Bake in the oven for 30 minutes until golden and cooked through.

- Serve hot with barbecued beans and a large mixed salad.

• From the Pie Shop

Serves 4

Cheese Tomato and Pesto Pies

Preparation time:
15 minutes
Cooking time:
20 minutes
To freeze:
Best frozen uncooked; open-freeze until firm, then pack in sealable freezer bags and freeze for up to 3 months

These tasty parcels are best served hot as they have the lovely, gooey quality that Mozzarella brings, but they can be eaten cold for quick lunches. Add more Mediterranean flavours with some sliced olives or capers, or try diced beetroot instead of tomatoes.

Speed tip: Ready-grated Cheddar is often no more expensive than buying a block so is worth keeping in the fridge for cooking

500g puff pastry, thawed if frozen
2 tbsp green pesto
4 tomatoes, sliced
100g Mozzarella cheese, cut into small dice
100g Cheddar cheese, grated
Freshly ground black pepper
Beaten egg, to glaze

To serve
Village Salad (page 131) or other large mixed salad

- Preheat the oven to 200°C/gas 6.

- Cut the pastry in quarters and roll out to four rectangles, about 16 x 20cm. Spread the pesto over one half of each rectangle, leaving a border round the three edges. Top with the tomatoes, then the cheeses. Season well.

- Brush the edges with beaten egg and fold the pastry over the filling to encase completely, pressing the edges well together, then roll over the edges and press firmly to seal completely. Transfer to a dampened sheet. Mark a lattice pattern on top of each with the back of a knife, taking care not to cut right through the pastry. Brush with beaten egg to glaze.

- Bake in the oven for about 20 minutes until puffy, crisp and golden.

- Serve with a large salad.

From the Kebab House

A kebab after a Friday night out is great but so often people eat them when they've already had far too much beer and don't really appreciate the flavours. Having them for a night *in*, instead, means you can savour every mouthful – and enjoy a beer or two without having to stagger home afterwards. Here I've recreated the fabulous donor – okay, not cooked on a spit, but the flavour and texture are great *and* you know it's made with all good things, freshly cooked, rather than one that may have been lurking in the shop for a dubious length of time!

Maybe you're a shish kebab person instead, enjoying cubes of tender meat, marinated then grilled so oozing flavour and juiciness, or colourful vegetable ones, fragrant with herbs and garlic. Either is perfect packed in pitta breads with some crisp salad.

The third kind are the koftas – cylinders of minced lamb flavoured with herbs and spices then grilled round skewers. Perfect with rice, cooling tzatsiki and a village salad topped with cubes of feta cheese.

Takeaway Tip

Feta cheese for the classic salad: Feta freezes really well so it's worth keep a vacuum-packed slab to hand. It can be cut into chunks whilst still frozen to scatter over a Village Salad (it thaws really quickly) when you don't want or need to use the whole block in one go.

CHAPTER 10

Preparation time:
10 minutes plus marinating
Cooking time:
6-8 minutes
To freeze:
Best eaten fresh

Serves 4

Shish Kebabs

3 tbsp olive oil
1 tbsp lemon juice
1 tsp dried oregano
1 garlic clove, crushed (or
    ½ tsp garlic purée)
Pinch of salt
Freshly ground black pepper
500g lamb neck fillets or
    diced leg, pork fillets or
    skinless chicken breasts,
    trimmed and cut into bite-
    sized pieces
1 red pepper, cut into bite-
    sized chunks
1 green pepper, cut into
    bite-sized chunks

To serve
Warm pitta breads, shredded
    lettuce, sliced tomatoes,
    cucumber and red onion,
    lemon wedges

I keep chicken breasts, pork and lamb neck fillets in the freezer as they're so versatile. These kebabs are quick and easy to prepare but are best left to marinate if you have time. For a change, try a dollop of hummus or mayonnaise spooned over in the pittas.

● Whisk the oil, lemon juice, oregano, garlic, salt and pepper in a large container with a lid. Add the lamb and toss well. If time, cover and marinate in the fridge for several hours.

● Preheat the grill. Drain the meat, reserving the marinade, and thread on soaked wooden or metal skewers, interspersed with pieces of pepper. Place on the grill rack.

● Brush with the reserved marinade. Grill for 6–8 minutes until cooked through and lightly golden, turning once and brushing with the remaining marinade during cooking.

● Remove from the skewers and pack in warm, split pitta breads, with the prepared salad ingredients. Serve with lemon wedges to squeeze over.

● From the Kebab House

Serves 4

Kofta Kebabs

Preparation time:
15 minutes
Cooking time:
10–12 minutes
To freeze:
Best eaten fresh but can be
cooked then removed from the
skewers and frozen for up to 3
months

Try serving these tubes of spicy meat with a chickpea salad for a change – drain a can of chickpeas and mix with chopped peppers, onion, garlic and plenty of fresh chopped coriander or parsley, simply dressed with lemon juice and olive oil.

- Preheat the grill. Mix all the kebab ingredients together with your hands, squeezing the mixture well to mix thoroughly.

- Divide into 8 equal pieces and shape each into a cylinder around the skewers, so they are about half the length of the sticks.

- Brush with oil and place on the grill rack. Grill for 10–12 minutes, turning once, until golden and cooked through.

- Serve with plain rice, tzatsiki and a village salad.

For the kebabs
500g lean minced lamb
2 large garlic cloves, crushed
    (or 2 tsp garlic purée)
1 small onion, grated
    (or 2 tsp onion granules or
    2 tsp onion purée)
2 tsp ground cumin
1 tbsp sweet paprika
½ tsp chilli powder
1 tsp dried oregano
2 tbsp chopped fresh or
    frozen coriander
Salt and freshly ground black
    pepper
1 egg, beaten
8 soaked wooden skewers
2 tbsp olive oil

To serve
Rice, Tzatsiki (page 130) and
    a Village Salad (page 131)

Preparation time:
10 minutes
Cooking time:
1 hour plus resting
To freeze:
Cut the cooked donor kebab in thin slices and interleave with pieces of baking parchment or clingfilm; freeze in a rigid container

500g lean minced lamb
1 garlic clove, crushed (or ½ tsp garlic purée)
1 small onion, grated (or 1 tsp onion granules)
Good pinch of chilli powder
1 tsp dried oregano
1 tsp dried mint
½ tsp salt
Good grinding of black pepper
A little sunflower oil

To serve
8 warm pitta breads, Tzatziki (page 130), shredded lettuce, sliced cucumber, sliced tomatoes and chilli sauce

Serves 4

Lamb Donor Kebabs

Putting the lamb loaf on a rack ensures that all the fat drips away like it does when on the spit in the kebab house. For a chicken donor, substitute chicken mince and use dried thyme instead of the oregano.

- Preheat the oven to 180°C/gas 4.

- Put the lamb in a large bowl. Mix together all the remaining ingredients except the oil and add to the lamb. Mix thoroughly with your hands, squeezing well together to combine completely. Shape into a squat, fat loaf 10–12 cm in diameter.

- Place the loaf on a rack set in a roasting tin. Brush with a little oil. Roast in the oven for 1 hour. Check half way through cooking and baste with any juices in the pan or brush with a little more sunflower oil.

- Remove from the oven, cover with foil and leave in a warm place to rest for at least 5–10 minutes whilst you warm and split the pittas and prepare the salad ingredients.

- Thinly slice the meat and serve in the pittas with tzatsiki, the salad ingredients and chilli sauce.

• From the Kebab House

Serves 4

Preparation time:
20 minutes
Cooking time:
8 minutes
To freeze:
Best eaten fresh

Vegetable Shish Kebabs

You can, of course, use other vegetables for this kebab but I find these make a delicious combination. Blanching them first ensures the vegetables remain moist and tender. You can also serve the kebabs on rice with thick slices of grilled halloumi cheese.

- Blanch the peppers, onion and courgettes in a pan of lightly salted boiling water for 2 minutes. Drain, rinse with cold water and drain again.

- Preheat the grill and line it with foil.

- Thread the vegetables alternately on 8 skewers with the mushrooms and bay leaves. Place on the lined grill rack.

- Mix together the oil, garlic and rosemary with a little salt and pepper. Brush all over the kebabs. Grill about 5mm from the heat source or cook on a hot griddle for about 8 minutes, turning once and brushing with more garlic oil during cooking, until tender and lightly golden at the edges.

- Serve in warm pitta breads with some shredded salad, and a good dollop of hummus.

1 small red pepper, deseeded and cut into 8 chunks
1 small yellow pepper, deseeded and cut into 8 chunks
1 red onion, quartered and separated into slices
1 small courgette, cut into 8 pieces
8 chestnut mushrooms
6 tbsp olive oil
2 garlic clove, crushed (or 1 tsp garlic purée)
1 tbsp fresh chopped rosemary
Salt and freshly ground black pepper

To serve
Warm pitta breads and shredded lettuce
1 small tub hummus

Serves 4

Tzatsiki

¼ cucumber, peeled and
   coarsely grated
200ml thick plain yoghurt
1 small garlic clove, crushed
   (or ½ tsp garlic purée)
1 tbsp dried mint
Salt and freshly ground black
   pepper

This is quite similar to the Indian raita but usually contains garlic
and, often, lemon juice. It is delicious as a dip with crudités or strips
of warm pitta bread for a starter or snack meal, or try it spooned
onto jacket-baked potatoes.

● Squeeze the cucumber to remove excess moisture. Place in a bowl
   with the remaining ingredients and mix well. Season to taste.

● Chill until ready to serve.

● From the Kebab House

Serves 4

Village Salad

Preparation time:
8 minutes
To freeze:
Not suitable for freezing

This is the perfect accompaniment to any of the kebabs in this section or try it with any of the chicken shack recipes on pages 99–111, or even the pies, particularly the Cheese, Tomato and Pesto Pies (page 123). For the record, it's good with grilled or roast meat or fish, too.

- Finely shred the cabbage, discarding the thick central core. Scatter all over a large platter. Finely shred the lettuce and scatter over the cabbage. Top with the tomatoes, cucumber, onion rings and olives, then crumble the cheese over the top in small pieces.

- Sprinkle with the oregano and some salt and lots of black pepper. Drizzle with the oil and vinegar to serve.

½ small white cabbage
½ small romaine lettuce
2 tomatoes cut into small wedges
5cm piece cucumber, diced
1 small red onion, thinly sliced
Handful of stoned black olives
75g feta cheese, crumbled
½ tsp dried oregano
Salt and freshly ground black pepper
3 tbsp olive oil
1 tbsp white wine vinegar

From the Thai Takeaway

CHAPTER
11

Thai food is increasingly popular in the UK. The wonderful thing is that, although a lot of it tastes quite fiery, the heat doesn't last so one can tolerate much more heat than with, say, Indian curries.

There are a few essential ingredients for these recipes – apart from the curry pastes – and they are Thai fish sauce (*nam pla*), lemon grass (a jar of purée is fine) and, of course, coconut milk. This has become very expensive over the past year because of poor coconut harvests. You may find it's a good idea to buy a box of coconut powder, which you reconstitute with water, instead. This will keep for ages in the cupboard. Thai fragrant rice is also different from basmati or other types of long-grain rice. It has a distinctive flavour and is served slightly sticky rather than fluffy with each grain separate. It's the perfect vehicle for soaking up all the lovely, runny coconut curry sauces. Thai curries tend to use quick-cook ingredients rather than the long, slow cooking needed for some Indian ones, so they are perfect to throw together for a meal in the evening with very little effort.

Takeaway Tip

Lowering fat: You may like to look for reduced-fat coconut milk (as it is quite high in saturated fat) but, beware, it tends to curdle slightly, particularly if you have vegetables in the dish. It doesn't alter the flavour though so the decision is yours!

Preparation time:
20 minutes
Cooking time:
20 minutes
To freeze:
Best eaten fresh but can be
frozen for up to 3 months in a
rigid container

Serves 4

Thai Red Beef Curry

2 tbsp sunflower oil
1 red onion, thinly sliced
500g lean frying steak or
   rump, trimmed and cut
   into very thin strips
3 tbsp Thai red curry paste
1 aubergine, cubed
2 potatoes, peeled and cut
   into chunks
400ml can of coconut milk
1 tbsp Thai fish sauce
1 tsp soft light brown sugar
2 courgettes, cut into
   chunks
2 tomatoes, quartered
2 handfuls of raw cashew
   nuts

To garnish
A few torn fresh coriander or
   basil leaves

To serve
Thai fragrant rice

By using a tender cut of beef, like frying steak or rump, you can make this very quickly. Galangal is the correct spice for this dish (and you can buy it in supermarkets if you wish) but ginger works just fine so saves on the expenditure.

- Heat the oil in a large saucepan. Add the onion and beef and stir-fry for 2 minutes.

- Stir in the curry paste and fry for 30 seconds.

- Add the aubergine, potatoes, coconut milk, fish sauce and brown sugar. Bring to the boil, then reduce the heat and simmer gently for 20 minutes or until the beef and vegetables are tender.

- Meanwhile steam or boil the courgettes for 3–4 minutes until just tender but still bright green. (You can spread them out in a steamer or metal colander, cover and place over the pan of rice to save fuel.) Drain, if necessary.

- Stir the courgettes, tomatoes and nuts into the curry and cook for 2 minutes just to heat through the tomato, but don't let it become completely soft.

- Taste and add more fish sauce, if necessary. Spoon over rice and garnish with a few torn coriander or basil leaves.

• From the Thai Takeaway

Serves 4

Preparation time:
20 minutes
Cooking time:
20 minutes
To freeze:
Best eaten fresh but can be
frozen for up to 3 months in a
rigid container

Thai Red Vegetable Curry

You can vary the vegetables according to what's in season. Make sure you get a variety of colour and texture though. The butternut squash adds the desired amount of sweetness but sweet potato would work just as well.

- Heat the oil in a large saucepan. Add the curry paste and fry for 30 seconds, stirring.

- Stir in the lemon grass then all the vegetables and turn to coat in the paste. Stir in the coconut milk and fish sauce. Bring to the boil, then reduce the heat, part-cover and simmer gently for about 20 minutes until the vegetables are tender.

- Gently stir in the tofu and heat through for 2 minutes.

- Spoon over fragrant rice and garnish with a few strips of fresh chilli (optional).

1 tbsp sunflower oil
2 tbsp Thai red curry paste
1 tsp lemon grass purée
1 bunch of spring onions, cut
  into short diagonal lengths
2 potatoes, peeled and cut
  into bite-sized chunks
½ small butternut squash,
  bite-sized chunks
2 red peppers, cut into
  chunks
100g green beans, trimmed
  and cut into short lengths
  (or use frozen)
400ml can of coconut milk
1 tbsp Thai fish sauce
1 block firm tofu, cubed

To garnish
1 red or green chilli,
  deseeded (if liked) and cut
  into very thin strips
  (optional)

To serve
Thai fragrant rice

Serves 4

Thai Green Chicken Curry

Preparation time:
10 minutes
Cooking time:
10 minutes
To freeze:
Best eaten fresh but can be
frozen for up to 3 months in a
rigid container

1 tbsp sunflower oil
1 onion, chopped (or a large
   handful of frozen chopped
   onion)
4 skinless chicken breasts,
   cut into chunks
3 tbsp Thai green curry paste
1 tbsp Thai fish sauce
1 tsp grated fresh root
   ginger (or ginger purée)
1 garlic clove, crushed (or
   ½ tsp garlic purée)
400ml can of coconut milk
150g green beans, trimmed
   and cut into short lengths

To garnish
1 green chilli, cut into thin
   shreds or a few chive
   stalks, optional

To serve
Thai fragrant rice

This is another good dish you can make with cooked, leftover chicken. Simply make the sauce, add the chicken and simmer for 3 minutes only until hot through. If you don't have enough meat, add a can of white beans or lentils as well.

- Heat the oil and fry the onion gently, stirring for 3 minutes until softened but not browned.

- Add the chicken and fry, stirring, until opaque. Stir in the curry paste and fry for 30 seconds, stirring.

- Add the remaining ingredients except the beans. Bring to the boil, then reduce the heat, part-cover and simmer for 10 minutes.

- Either steam the beans, spread out evenly in a steamer or colander over the curry or place over the rice when you cook it just until the beans are tender but still bright green, about 5 minutes.

- Stir the beans into the curry and serve spooned over fragrant rice then garnished with some thin shreds of chilli or a few chive stalks, if using.

• From the Thai Takeaway

Serves 4

Pad Thai

Preparation time:
10 minutes
Cooking time:
7 minutes
To freeze:
Best eaten fresh

There are many versions of the national noodle dish but this is one of the simplest. Substitute raw tiger prawns for the chicken for a special occasion. Traditionally it has a teaspoon or more of palm or brown sugar added but I prefer it without.

- Cook the noodles according to packet directions. Drain and set aside.

- Heat the oil in a large pan or wok. Add the chicken and stir-fry for 2 minutes.

- Add the spring onions, pepper and chilli and stir-fry a further 2 minutes.

- Stir in the beansprouts for 1 minute to soften slightly.

- Stir in the noodles and all the flavourings except the eggs and the garnish ingredients. Toss and stir until blended and hot through.

- Beat the eggs well in a jug. Slowly drizzle them all over the top in a thin stream and leave to cook for a minute or two so they set in strands. Toss gently.

- Pile in bowls and top with the chopped peanuts.

- Serve with lime wedges to squeeze over and the Thai salad.

250g wide ribbon rice
noodles (or thinner brown
rice ones)
3 tbsp sunflower oil
4 small chicken breasts, cut
into thick diagonal slices
1 bunch of spring onions, cut
into diagonal short lengths
1 red pepper, thinly sliced
(optional)
1 small red chilli, deseeded
(if liked) and finely
chopped (or $\frac{1}{2}$ tsp dried
chilli flakes or chilli purée)
200g fresh beansprouts
3 tbsp oyster sauce
2 tbsp soy sauce
1 tbsp Thai fish sauce
2 tbsp chopped fresh or
frozen coriander
4 eggs

To garnish
Lime wedges and a handful
of toasted, unsalted
peanuts, chopped

To serve
Thai-dressed Green Salad
(page 143)

Preparation time:
15 minutes
Cooking time:
4 minutes
To freeze:
Best eaten fresh but can be
frozen for up to 2 months in a
rigid container

Serves 4

Thai-style Crab Cakes

170g can of white crabmeat
    or 120g seafood sticks
175g white fish fillet (coley,
    pollock or any sustainable
    fish), thawed, if frozen,
    skinned
1 tbsp Thai fish sauce
2 spring onions, finely
    chopped
1 tsp lemon grass purée
1 tsp grated fresh root
    ginger (or ginger purée)
$\frac{1}{2}$ tsp dried basil
4 tbsp plain flour
1 egg, beaten
Sunflower oil

To serve
Sweet Chilli Dipping Sauce
    (page 141) or use bought,
    and Thai Rocket and
    Cashew Salad (page 142)

To make these less expensive, I've used some crabmeat and some flaked white fish. The result is still really tasty and I don't think many people would even know. The seafood sticks are an even more economical version and still delicious!

• Drain the liquor from the crabmeat, if using, into a shallow dish. Alternatively, if using seafood sticks, put 4 tbsp water in the dish. Add the fish fillet. Cover with a plate and microwave on HIGH for 2½–3 minutes until just cooked through. Alternatively, place on a covered plate over a pan of simmering water for about 6 minutes. Drain.

• Flake the crab or mash the crabsticks so they break into shreds. Add to the fish with the spring onions, lemon grass, ginger and basil and mix well. Stir in the flour, then the beaten egg to bind the mixture together.

• With wet hands, shape the mixture into 8 small cakes. If time, place on baking parchment on a plate and chill for at least 30 minutes (or overnight if easier).

• When ready to serve, heat about 5mm sunflower oil in a large frying pan and shallow-fry the cakes for about 2 minutes on each side until golden brown. Drain on kitchen paper. Serve warm with sweet chilli sauce and Thai salad.

• From the Thai Takeaway

Serves 4

Thai Chicken Satay with Crunchy Peanut Sauce

Preparation time:
10 minutes plus marinating
Cooking time:
8 minutes
To freeze:
Best eaten fresh

Some satay dishes are simply pieces of chicken brushed with a little of the peanut sauce then grilled. Thai chicken is marinated first, which adds a superb flavour and is well worth the extra little bit of effort involved.

- Prepare the chicken. Put all the ingredients for the chicken, except the chicken itself, in a large, shallow sealable container. Add the chicken slices and toss gently with your hands so they are well coated. Cover and place in the fridge to marinate for several hours or overnight.

- When nearly ready to serve, make the sauce. Put all the ingredients in small saucepan and heat, stirring, until the peanut butter has melted. Bring to the boil, then simmer for 1 minute.

- Preheat the grill. Thread each strip of chicken on a soaked wooden skewer, concertina fashion. Grill about 5cm from the heat, in batches if necessary, for 4 minutes each side until cooked through, brushing with any remaining marinade once or twice during cooking.

- Serve the skewers on rice noodles with the hot peanut sauce and a Thai-dressed green salad.

For the chicken
2 tbsp sunflower oil
1 tsp lemon grass purée
1 garlic clove, crushed (or ½ tsp garlic purée)
1 tsp grated fresh root ginger (or ginger purée)
2 tbsp light soy sauce
1 tsp ground turmeric
1 tsp ground cumin
¼ tsp chilli powder
4 skinless chicken breasts, each cut into 6 strips lengthways
24 wooden skewers, soaked

For the peanut sauce
175ml water
2 spring onions, finely chopped
8 tbsp crunchy peanut butter
1 tbsp clear honey
2 tbsp light soy sauce
1 tsp dried chilli flakes

To serve
Rice noodles, dressed with a splash of sesame oil and lime juice, and a large Thai-dressed Green Salad (page 143)

Preparation time:
5 minutes
Cooking time:
5 minutes
To freeze:
Best eaten fresh

Serves 4

Thai Noodles

4 nests of medium egg
  noodles
1 tbsp soy sauce
1 tbsp sesame oil
1 tbsp lime juice
2 tsp clear honey
1 tsp Thai fish sauce
1 tsp grated fresh root
  ginger (or ginger purée)
1 tsp chopped lemon grass
  (or lemon grass purée)
1 tsp dried chilli flakes
1 tbsp chopped fresh horapa
  or basil (or 1 tsp dried
  basil)
1 tbsp chopped fresh or
  frozen coriander
A few sesame seeds, to
  garnish

These make a quick and tasty snack on their own or you can throw
in some cooked peas or sweetcorn with perhaps some peeled
prawns or chopped cooked chicken to create an easy meal to serve
with a Thai-dressed Green Salad (page 143).

• Cook the noodles according to the packet directions. Drain and
  return to the pan.

• Whisk all the other ingredients together. Pour over the noodles
  and toss over a gentle heat until well coated and heated through.

• Pile into bowls and sprinkle with sesame seeds. Serve hot.

• From the Thai Takeaway

Serves 4

Sweet Chilli Dipping Sauce

Preparation time:
5 minutes
Cooking time:
2–3 minutes
To freeze:
Not suitable for freezing

This is a delicious, more nutritious version of the clear, reddish sweet chilli sauce you buy. If you like it, make a double batch and store it in the fridge for up to 2 weeks. It's perfect with grilled crab cakes, prawns, chicken, wraps – anything that requires a bit of heat !

- Mix the passata, chilli, garlic, ketchup, fish sauce and honey together in a small saucepan and heat through, stirring.

- Blend the cornflour with the water and stir in. Bring to the boil and cook for 1 minute, stirring until slightly thickened. Spoon into small pots and leave to cool.

150ml passata
2 tsp dried chilli flakes
1 garlic clove, crushed (or ½ tsp garlic purée)
2 tbsp tomato ketchup
2 tsp Thai fish sauce
1 tbsp clear honey
2 tsp cornflour
3 tbsp water

Serves 4

Thai Rocket and Cashew Salad

50g rocket
50g baby spinach or ¼ head Chinese leaves, shredded
2 spring onions, cut into short, thin shreds
1 red pepper, cut into very thin strips
1 large handful of toasted, unsalted cashew nuts

For the dressing
2 tbsp sunflower oil
2 tsp Thai fish sauce
1 tbsp lime or lemon juice
1 tsp lemon grass purée (or grated lemon rind)
2 tsp clear honey
½ tsp dried chilli flakes
1 tbsp chopped fresh or frozen coriander

This is delicious served with the crab cakes or chicken satay but try it, too, with fresh grilled tuna or chicken, brushed with a little soy sauce, honey and garlic before grilling. To toast raw nuts, toss them in a hot non-stick frying pan briefly until browned.

• Wash and dry the leaves and place in large bowl. Scatter the spring onions, pepper and nuts over.

• Whisk the dressing ingredients together and pour over the salad. Toss gently. Pile into small bowls, making sure you have some nuts, pepper and onions on top.

• From the Thai Takeaway

Serves 4

Thai-dressed Green Salad

Preparation time:
5 minutes
To freeze:
Not suitable for freezing

This is crisp and light with just the right amount of salty-sweetness to go with any Thai main course. The same dressing is good spooned over sliced tomatoes, radishes and onions, too. Thai basil, horapa, is sometimes available, so do use it if you can find it.

3 tbsp sunflower oil
1 tbsp light soy sauce
1 tbsp lime juice
2 tsp soft light brown sugar
Good pinch of dried chilli
  flakes
1 tbsp shredded fresh basil
  leaves
100g mixed salad leaves

- Whisk all the ingredients except the salad leaves in a salad bowl.

- Just before serving, add the salad leaves to the dressing and toss gently until every leaf is glistening.

From the Japanese Noodle and Sushi Bar

Most Japanese food is low in fat (great!) and a fabulous balance of mind-blowing textures, tastes and colours. Sushi, for instance, looks amazing with the deep pink of the salmon, the deep green of the nori wraps, the sticky white rice, and so on. It is delicious as a takeaway or to choose to eat in a sushi bar but it's also great fun to make at home and really is far simpler than you might think. It may not be something you'd want to do every day but, if you're feeling creative one weekend, it's the perfect Saturday night treat – with some chilled white wine.

I've also created versions of some of your favourite noodle main meal soup dishes that you would find in some of the chain restaurants and takeaway bars using ramen and udon noodles (available in all good supermarkets) plus crispy vegetable tempura and simple marinated dishes like chicken yakitori and salmon teryaki, which are so easy to make you'll be amazed! The key to all Japanese cooking is to use very fresh ingredients and to keep the flavours simple, clean and fresh.

> ### Takeaway Tip
> **Japanese soy sauce**: If you like Japanese food, it's worth buying a bottle of Tamari – Japanese soy sauce – as it's less salty and more flavourful than ordinary Chinese dark soy, which makes it good as a dipping sauce as well as a seasoning.

Preparation time:
15 minutes including soaking
Cooking time:
6–8 minutes
To freeze:
Best eaten fresh

Serves 4

Miso Soup

2 x 10cm piece wakame (dried seaweed)
1 heaped tbsp dried shiitake mushrooms
750ml lukewarm water
2 spring onions, cut into short, thin shreds
1 large carrot, cut into short, very thin matchsticks
1 tbsp vegetable stock powder or concentrate
2 tbsp red or white miso paste
½ block tofu, drained and cut into small cubes

Miso paste keeps for ages in the fridge. For a basic soup, simply add the chopped spring onions and wakame to the stock. I've created a more substantial one and you can add cubes of fresh tuna, salmon or even cooked chicken instead of the tofu if you prefer.

- Soak the wakame and shiitake mushrooms in 300ml of the water for 15 minutes.

- Drain the liquid into a saucepan. Lift out the wakame and cut out any thick stalk. Cut into neat pieces.

- Put the wakame, soaked mushrooms, remaining water, spring onions, carrot and stock powder or concentrate in the saucepan with the soaking water. Bring to the boil, then reduce the heat, cover and simmer gently for 6–8 minutes until the carrot is tender.

- Blend the miso paste with a ladleful of the soup liquid until smooth, then pour into the pan. Add the tofu. Stir gently and heat through but do not boil.

- Ladle into warm soup bowls and serve.

• From the Japanese Noodle and Sushi Bar

Serves 4

Preparation time:
20 minutes plus soaking
Cooking time:
8 minutes
To freeze:
Best eaten fresh

Chicken and Vegetable Rice Noodle Soup

The following two main meal soups are nutritious and filling. Add other vegetables or some cubes of tofu instead of chicken for a vegetarian option. For a lower-fat option, choose reduced-fat coconut milk but add at the end and just heat through.

- Soak the wakame and the shiitake mushrooms in 300ml of the water for 15 minutes. Lift out the wakame and cut out any thick stalk then shred the seaweed, if necessary.

- Place in a large pot with all the ingredients (including the soaking water) except the noodles. Bring to the boil, then reduce the heat and simmer for 8 minutes. Taste and season, if necessary.

- Meanwhile, soak the noodles in boiling water for 4 minutes or according to the packet directions.

- Drain the noodles and place in four large soup bowls. Ladle the soup over and serve garnished with coriander leaves, with chilli flakes to sprinkle over, if using.

2 x 10cm pieces wakame
2 heaped tbsp dried shiitake mushrooms
600ml lukewarm water
4 spring onions, chopped
1 red pepper, cut into thin strips
1 carrot, peeled and cut into ribbons with a potato peeler
1 small can of bamboo shoots, drained
4 small skinless chicken breasts, cut into thick diagonal slices
400ml can of coconut milk
1 tsp grated fresh root ginger (or ginger purée)
1 garlic clove, crushed (or ½ tsp garlic purée)
1 tsp lemon grass purée
2 tbsp chopped fresh or frozen coriander, plus a few leaves to garnish (optional)
1 tbsp lime juice
1 tbsp vegetable stock powder or concentrate
Salt and freshly ground black pepper
4 slabs dried rice noodles (about 200g)

To serve
Dried chilli flakes (optional)

Preparation time:
10 minutes
Cooking time:
10 minutes
To freeze:
Best eaten fresh

Serves 4

Seafood Ramen Noodle Soup

250g dried ramen noodles
250g piece thick salmon
  fillet, skinned and cut into
  quarters
A little sunflower oil
1.2 litres water
2 tbsp vegetable stock
  concentrate
2 tbsp tamari (or light soy
  sauce)
2 tsp soft light brown sugar
3 tbsp mirin (or dry sherry)
4 spring onions, chopped
1 yellow pepper, finely sliced
2 heads of pak choi, cut into
  thick shreds
1 courgette, cut into
  matchsticks
4 radishes, sliced
100g raw, peeled king
  prawns, thawed, if frozen
4 baby squid cut into rings
  or 8 crab sticks, halved
  lengthways
1 tbsp white miso paste

To serve
Sweet Chilli Sauce (page 141
  or use bought) or chilli oil
  (optional)

Have fun with experimenting with different vegetables, chicken, or even thinly sliced fillet steak for a delicious supper. I add miso paste to enhance the flavour but omit if you prefer and season with tamari. Use dashi powder instead of stock concentrate, if you can find it.

- Preheat the grill.

- Cook the noodles according to the packet directions. Drain.

- Brush the salmon with the oil and grill for 3–4 minutes until just cooked through. Do not turn over. Set aside and keep warm.

- Meanwhile, put the remaining ingredients except the prawns, squid or crabsticks and miso paste in a large pan. Bring to the boil, then reduce the heat and simmer for 2 minutes.

- Add the prawns and squid or crab sticks and simmer for a further 2 minutes.

- Blend a ladleful of the stock with the miso paste until smooth. Pour back into the pan and stir gently. Taste and add more tamari, if necessary.

- Pile the noodles in large soup bowls. Add a piece of salmon to each bowl. Ladle the soup over.

- Serve straight away with sweet chilli sauce or chilli oil to drizzle over, if using.

• From the Japanese Noodle and Sushi Bar

Serves 4

Preparation time:
10 minutes
Cooking time:
8 minutes
To freeze:
Best eaten fresh

Salmon Teryaki

Skinless chicken breasts can be prepared in exactly the same way for another delicious, quick midweek meal. If you really can't be bothered to cook the noodles, buy a large pack of ready-to-use ones.

Speed tip: Use bought sticky teriyaki sauce instead of making your own and simply heat it up, then add the salmon

- Put the tamari, lime juice, ginger, garlic, chilli and honey in a frying pan, stir well, bring to the boil, then boil for 2–3 minutes until syrupy.

- Meanwhile, place the salmon on oiled foil on the grill rack, skin-side up and grill for 3 minutes until the skin is crispy. Carefully turn the fish over and grill a further 1 minute.

- Place the salmon in the hot sticky sauce, and spoon the sticky glaze over it until it glistens all over.

- Meanwhile, cook the noodles according to the packet directions. Drain and toss in the sesame oil, if using.

- Serve the fish on the udon noodles with a Japanese-style mixed vegetable salad with pickled ginger served separately.

6 tbsp tamari (or light soy sauce)
2 tbsp lime juice
2 tsp grated fresh root ginger (or ginger purée)
2 garlic cloves, crushed (or 1 tsp garlic purée)
1 red chilli, deseeded (if liked) and chopped (or $\frac{1}{2}$ tsp dried chilli flakes or chilli purée)
3 tbsp clear honey
4 chunky pieces of salmon fillet (about 150g each)
A little sunflower oil, for greasing
175–250g (2–3 bundles) dried Udon noodles (depending on appetites)
1–2 tbsp sesame oil (optional)

To serve
Japanese-style Mixed Vegetable Salad (page 154)

reparation time:
15 minutes plus marinating
Cooking time:
15 minutes
To freeze:
Best eaten fresh

Serves 4

Chicken Yakitori

4 tbsp tamari (or light soy
   sauce)
2 tbsp mirin (or dry sherry)
1 tbsp sunflower oil
½ tsp grated fresh root
   ginger (or ginger purée)
1 tbsp soft light brown sugar
Freshly ground black pepper
4 skinless chicken breasts,
   cut into small chunks
1 green pepper, cut into
   small chunks
1 courgette, cut into thick
   slices
4 thick spring onions, cut
   into short, diagonal
   lengths
8–12 soaked wooden
   skewers

To serve
Egg Fried Rice (page 59),
   flavoured with tamari
   rather than dark soy, if
   you prefer, and Japanese
   Daikon and Carrot Salad
   (page 155)

Prepare the chicken in the morning ready to grill quickly when you get home. Alternatively set it to soak the minute you get in and go and have a bath or watch your favourite TV programme while you wait! Try mushrooms or mangetout instead of courgettes or onions.

- Mix together the tamari, mirin, oil, ginger, sugar and plenty of pepper. Put the chicken in a shallow dish. Pour the marinade over and toss well. Cover and chill for at least 1 hour (or longer if more convenient).

- Preheat the grill.

- Lift the chicken out of the marinade and thread on soaked wooden skewers alternately with the vegetables.

- Grill the chicken for about 15 minutes, turning and brushing with any remaining marinade once or twice during cooking.

- Serve with egg fried rice and Japanese daikon and carrot salad.

• From the Japanese Noodle and Sushi Bar

Serves 4

Vegetable Tempura

Preparation time:
25 minutes
Cooking time:
16 minutes
To freeze:
Best eaten fresh

Use different vegetables as you like. I use self-raising flour as I find it gives extra crunch but use plain if you prefer. Make sure you fry just a few pieces at a time and reheat the oil between batches, skimming off any stray bits of crispy batter.

Speed tip: Use thawed, frozen casserole vegetables and don't bother to blanch before dipping in the batter

- Mix the dipping sauce ingredients together in a small bowl, stirring until the honey dissolves. Set aside.

- Blanch all the prepared vegetables in a large pan of boiling water for 2 minutes. Drain and dry thoroughly on kitchen paper.

- Put the vegetables in large bowl. Sprinkle with the 4 tbsp cornflour and toss to coat.

- Heat the sunflower oil for deep-frying in a large pan or deep-fryer until a drop of the batter sizzles and rises to the surface immediately (or to 190°C).

- While it's heating, quickly make the batter. Mix the two flours in a bowl with the salt then whisk in the cold sparkling water. Don't overmix; it doesn't matter if there are a few little lumps.

- When the oil is hot, add the vegetables to the batter and toss so all are thinly coated. Cook about a quarter of the vegetables at a time, dropping each piece individually into the hot oil. Fry for about 4 minutes until the batter is crisp and pale straw-coloured. Remove with a slotted spoon and drain on kitchen paper. Keep warm while you cook the remainder in the same way, reheating the oil between batches. Serve hot with the dipping source.

For the dipping sauce
1 tsp grated fresh root
    ginger (or ginger purée)
1 spring onion, finely
    chopped
1 tbsp clear honey
½ tsp dried chilli flakes
4 tbsp tamari (or light soy
    sauce)

For the vegetables
½ daikon or 1 large turnip,
    cut into short, thick sticks
1 large carrot, quartered
    crossways then in quarters
    lengthways
1 courgette, cut into thick
    slices
½ small cauliflower, cut into
    small florets
1 red or green pepper, cut
    into bite-sized chunks
4 tbsp cornflour

For the batter
75g self-raising flour
75g cornflour
½ tsp salt
200ml ice cold sparkling
    mineral water
Sunflower oil for deep-frying

Preparation time:
40 minutes

Cooking time:
15 minutes plus standing and cooling

To freeze:
Best eaten fresh

Serves 4

Mixed Sushi Platter

For the sushi rice
250g sushi rice
3 tbsp rice vinegar, plus a
　splash
2 tsp caster sugar
2 tsp sesame oil
½ tsp salt

For the fillings and toppings
1 small avocado
4cm piece cucumber
½ small carrot
2 spring onions
2 nori wraps (dried seaweed)
75g cooked, peeled cold
　water prawns, thawed if
　frozen
1 slice smoked salmon
Sesame, nigella or black
　onion seeds

Sushi is fantastic to eat and fun to make. Ideally it should be served in bento boxes – individual lacquered boxes with lids – but, unless you have some to hand, plates or small trays will do just fine! Experiment with different fillings – even drained canned tuna works!

- Cook the sushi rice according to the packet directions, leaving to stand, covered, for 20 minutes.

- Mix the remaining rice ingredients together and pour over the rice. Toss well, then leave to cool.

- Halve the avocado and remove the stone. Peel the fruit, then cut into thin slices. Toss in a splash of rice vinegar to prevent browning.

- Cut 2 thin slices off the cucumber and reserve for garnish. Peel the remainder, cut in half and remove the seeds with a teaspoon. Cut the cucumber into short, thin sticks.

- Peel the carrot and cut into thin ribbons with a potato peeler.

- Slice the white end of the spring onions into thin diagonal slices. Cut the green end into very thin strips.

- Place half a nori sheet on a sushi mat – or a square of foil – with the long edge facing you. Spread the surface fairly thinly with ⅛ of the sushi rice, leaving a 2cm strip of nori uncovered, furthest from you.

- Mark a line across the centre of the rice. Lay some cucumber and

• From the Japanese Noodle and Sushi Bar

carrot all across that line. Use the mat or foil to help, start to roll the sushi away from you firmly, checking that the roll is tucking under as it rolls. Dampen the end strip of nori, so it sticks when finally rolled.

- Make another roll in the same way, then make 2 more but filling with some of the avocado and about half of the prawns. You should have used half the rice, too. Wrap each roll in clingfilm and chill until ready to serve.

- To make the remaining sushi (nigiri sushi), squeeze and shape the remaining rice into 12 little rectangles, with wetted hands. Top with a strip of smoked salmon or a slice of avocado, cut to fit, or a row of prawns. Garnish these with seeds, tiny strips of spring onion or triangles of cucumber. Transfer to a tray or plate and chill until ready to serve.

- Remove the clingfilm from the nori rolls (maki sushi) and cut each into 6 pieces. Arrange all the sushi on individual serving platters (or one large one) with tiny dishes of wasabi paste, pickled ginger and tamari to add to each morsel before eating.

Preparation time:
15 minutes
To freeze:
Not suitable for freezing

Serves 4

Japanese-style Mixed Vegetable Salad

1 red pepper, finely sliced
1 yellow pepper, finely sliced
2 celery sticks, cut into matchsticks
¼ cucumber, cut into matchsticks
1 carrot, cut into matchsticks
2 spring onions, chopped
1 tbsp tamari (or light soy sauce)
1½ tbsp rice vinegar (or white wine vinegar)
1 tsp soft light brown sugar
½ small garlic clove, crushed (or ¼ tsp garlic purée)
2 tbsp pickled ginger, chopped

Vary the ingredients according to what's available, thinking about colour and texture. Pink pickled ginger is pleasantly sweet but the white can be rather salty. If you prefer it sweeter, soak it in a little warm water with a spoonful of sugar in it for 5 minutes, then drain.

- Put all the prepared vegetables, except half the chopped spring onion, in a salad bowl. Reserve the remaining spring onion for garnish.

- Whisk the tamari, vinegar, sugar and garlic together and pour over. Add half the ginger. Toss gently. The vegetables should be only lightly flavoured with the dressing, not soaked!

- Mix together the remaining ginger and the reserved chopped spring onion and put a small pile on top of the salad to garnish.

Tip: Store the remaining pickled ginger in a clean screw-topped jar in the fridge or freeze in ice cube trays then tip into a sealable freezer bag and store for up to 3 months.

• From the Japanese Noodle and Sushi Bar

Serves 4

Preparation time:
10 minutes
To freeze:
Not suitable for freezing

Japanese Daikon and Carrot Salad

Kouhaku Namasu in Japanese, which means red and white salad. If you can't get daikon or turnips, celeriac makes a delicious alternative, but drop the matchsticks into water with a tablespoon of lemon juice to prevent discolouration until ready to finish.

Ingredients:
½ daikon or 2 large turnips
2 carrots
2 tbsp mirin (or dry sherry)
2 tbsp rice vinegar (or white wine vinegar)
1 tbsp soft light brown sugar
¼ tsp salt

- Peel and cut the daikon or turnips and the carrots into thin matchsticks or ribbons using a potato peeler. Place in a bowl.

- Whisk the remaining ingredients together and pour over the salad. Toss well and chill until ready to serve.

Index

Baked Vegetable Pilau Rice, 42
Barbecued Beans, 108
Basic Pizza Dough, 68
Beansprout and Pepper Salad, 61
beef
    Beef with Mushrooms and Oyster
        Sauce, 54
    Classic Hamburgers with All the
        Trimmings, 90
    Double Cheese Burgers, 91
    Ginger Beef with Mangetout, 55
    Keema Curry with Peas, Steak,
        Guinness and Stilton Pies, 117
    Steak and Onion Pasties, 116
    Thai Red Beef Curry, 134
Beer-battered Fish, 81
Bombay Aloo, 36
bread
    Quick Naan, 43
burgers
    Chicken and Bacon Burgers, 92
    Classic Hamburgers with All the
        Trimmings, 90
    Crispy Fillet Burger with Pepper
        Mayonnaise, 105
    Double Cheese Burgers, 91
    Fish Fillet Burgers, 95
    Sausage Burgers with Mushrooms
        and Apple, 93

Veggie Burgers, 94

Calzone, 74
Cheese, Tomato and Pesto Pies, 123
chicken
    Chicken and Bacon Burgers, 92
    Chicken Chow Mein, 52
    Chicken and Mushroom Pies, 120
    Chicken Nuggets with Barbecue
        Dipping Sauce, 103
    Chicken and Sweetcorn Soup, 46
    Chicken Tikka, 23
    Chicken Tikka Masala, 21
    Chicken and Vegetable Rice Noodle
        Soup, 147
    Chicken Yakitori, 150
    Chilli Chicken Salad Wrap, 104
    Chinese Chicken Curry, 51
    Crispy Fillet Burger with Pepper
        Mayonnaise, 105
    Oven-fried Chicken, 100
    Pad Thai, 137
    Quick Chicken Madras, 22
    Savoury-coated Crispy Fried
        Chicken, 101
    Smoky Glazed Chicken Wings, 102
    Tandoori Chicken, 20
    Thai Chicken Satay with Crunchy
        Peanut Sauce, 139

Thai Green Chicken Curry, 136
Chilli Chicken Salad Wrap, 104
Chinese Chicken Curry, 51
Chinese Spare Ribs, 50
chips
    Chips, 80
    Matchstick French Fries, 96
Classic Battered Fish and Chips, 80
Classic Hamburgers with All the
    Trimmings, 90
Coleslaw, 106
conversions 17
Cornish Pasties, 114
Crispy Fillet Burger with Pepper
    Mayonnaise, 105
Crispy Seaweed, 63
Cucumber Raita, 34
curry
    Bombay Aloo, 36
    Chicken Tikka Masala, 21
    Chinese Chicken Curry, 51
    Keema Curry with Peas, 26
    Lamb Biryani, 28
    Lamb Korma, 30
    Lamb Rogan Josh, 29
    Mixed Vegetable Curry, 37
    Palak Gosht, 27
    Pork Vindaloo, 25
    Quick Chicken Madras, 22
    Quick Prawn Curry, 24
    Sag Aloo, 35
    Thai Green Chicken Curry, 136
    Thai Red Beef Curry, 134
    Thai Red Vegetable Curry, 135

Double Cheese Burgers, 91

Dough Balls, 77
duck
    Peking Duck, 53

East End-style Pie and Liquor, 118
Easy Pickled Eggs, 86
eggs
    Easy Pickled Eggs, 86
    Egg Foo Yung, 48
    Egg Fried Rice, 59
equipment, 11

Fast Flatbread Pizza, 67
fish
    Beer-battered Fish, 81
    Classic Battered Fish and Chips, 80
    Fish Fillet Burgers, 95
    Mixed Sushi Platter, 152
    Oven-baked Crumb-coated Fish
        and Chips, 82
    Prawn Toasts, 57
    Quick Fish Cakes, 83
    Salmon Teryaki, 149
    Seafood Ramen Noodle Soup, 148
    Thai-style Crab Cakes, 138
Fluffy Mash, 107
Four Seasons Pizza, 72
freezing, 15

Giant Sausage Rolls, 122
Ginger Beef with Mangetout, 55
Golden Oven Wedges, 111

hygiene, 14

Indian Carrot Salad, 40

Instant Dal, 38
Italian Salad, 76

Jacket Potatoes with Soured Cream
    and Chives, 110
Japanese Cucumber and Wakame Salad,
Japanese Daikon and Carrot Salad, 155
Japanese-style Mixed Vegetable Salad, 154

kebabs
    Kofta Kebabs, 127
    Lamb Donor Kebabs, 128
    Shish Kebabs, 126
    Vegetable Shish Kebabs, 129
Keema Curry with Peas, 26
Kofta Kebabs, 127

lamb
    Cornish Pasties, 114
    Kofta Kebabs, 127
    Lamb Biryani, 28
    Lamb Doner Kebabs, 128
    Lamb Korma, 30
    Lamb and Mint Pies with Leeks and
        Carrots, 115
    Lamb Rogan Josh, 29
    Palak Gosht, 27
    Shish Kebabs, 126

Masoor Dal, 39
Matchstick French Fries, 96
Mini Vegetable Samosas, 32
Miso Soup, 146
Mixed Sushi Platter, 152
Mixed Vegetable Curry, 37
Mushy Peas, 85

noodles
    Chicken Chow Mein, 52
    Chicken and Vegetable Rice Noodle
        Soup, 147
    Thai Noodles, 140
    Pad Thai, 137
    Szechuan Spicy Peanut Noodles with
        Vegetables, 58

Onion Bhajis, 31
Oven-baked Crumb-coated Fish and
    Chips, 82
Oven-fried Chicken, 100

Pad Thai, 137
Palak Gosht, 27
Peking Duck, 53
Pig in a Crispy Blanket, 84
pies
    Cheese, Tomato and Pesto Pies, 123
    Chicken and Mushroom Pies, 120
    Cornish Pasties, 114
    East End-style Pie and Liquor, 118
    Lamb and Mint Pies with Leeks and
        Carrots, 115
    Steak, Guinness and Stilton Pies, 117
    Steak and Onion Pasties, 116
Pilau Rice, Simple, 41
pizza dough
    Basic Pizza Dough, 68
pizzas
    Deep-pan Filled Crust Pizza, 72
    Fast Flatbread Pizza, 67
    Four Seasons Pizza, 72
    Pizza Fiorentina, 70
    Pizza Napolitana, 69

Quick Pan Pizza, 66
Spicy Meat Feast Pizza, 71
What's in My Fridge Stuffed Pizza 75
pork
    Chinese Spare Ribs, 50
    Egg Foo Young, 48
    Giant Sausage Rolls, 122
    Pig in a Crispy Blanket, 84
    Pork Vindaloo, 25
    Sausage Burgers with Mushrooms and
        Apple, 93
    Sweet and Sour Pork, 49
    Wonton Soup, 47
potatoes
    Bombay Aloo, 36
    Fluffy Mash, 107
    Golden Oven Wedges, 111
    Jacket Potatoes with Soured Cream
        and Chives, 110
    Matchstick French Fries, 96
    Sag Aloo, 35
prawns
    Prawns with Cashew Nuts, 56
    Prawn Toasts, 57
    Quick Prawn Curry, 24

Quick Chicken Madras, 22
Quick Fish Cakes, 83
Quick Naan, 43
Quick Pan Pizza, 66
Quick Prawn Curry, 24
Quick Tartare Sauce, 87
Quick Vegetable Stir-fry, 60

rice
    Baked Vegetable Pilau Rice, 42

Egg Fried Rice, 59
Simple Pilau Rice, 41
Roasted Corn Cobs, 109
Root Crisps, 97

Sag Aloo, 35
salads
    Beansprout and Pepper Salad, 61
    Chilli Chicken Salad Wrap, 104
    Coleslaw, 106
    Indian Carrot Salad, 40
    Italian Salad, 76
    Japanese Daikon and Carrot Salad, 145
    Japanese-style Mixed Vegetable
        Salad, 144
    Thai Rocket and Cashew Salad, 142
    Thai-dressed Green Salad, 143
    Tzatsiki, 13
    Village Salad, 131
Salmon Teryaki, 149
sauces
    Quick Tartare Sauce, 87
    Sweet Chilli Dipping Sauce, 141
Sausage Burgers with Mushrooms
    and Apple, 93
Savoury-coated Crispy Fried Chicken, 101
Seafood Ramen Noodle Soup, 148
Shish Kebabs, 126
Simple Pilau Rice, 41
Smoky Glazed Chicken Wings, 102
soups
    Chicken and Sweetcorn Soup, 46
    Chicken and Vegetable Rice Noodle
        Soup, 147
    Miso Soup, 146
    Seafood Ramen Noodle Soup, 148

Wonton Soup, 47
Spicy Meat Feast Pizza, 71
spinach
    Sag Aloo, 35
Spring Rolls, 62
Steak, Guinness and Stilton Pies, 117
Steak and Onion Pasties, 116
storecupboard, 12
Sweet Chilli Dipping Sauce, 141
sweetcorn
    Chicken and Sweetcorn Soup, 46
    Roasted Corn Cobs, 108
Sweet and Sour Pork, 49
Szechuan Spicy Peanut Noodles with
    Vegetables, 58

Tandoori Chicken, 20
Tartare Sauce, Quick, 87
Thai
    Thai Chicken Satay with Crunchy
        Peanut Sauce, 139
    Thai-dressed Green Salad, 143
    Thai Green Chicken Curry, 136
    Thai Noodles, 140
    Thai Red Beef Curry, 134
    Thai Red Vegetable Curry, 135
    Thai Rocket and Cashew Salad, 142
    Thai-style Crab Cakes, 137

tofu
    Thai Red Vegetable Curry, 135
Tzatsiki, 130

vegetable dishes
    Barbecued Beans, 108
    Beansprout and Pepper Salad, 61
    Calzone, 74
    Crispy Seaweed, 63
    Four Seasons Pizza, 72
    Japanese-style Mixed Vegetable Salad,
        154
    Mini Vegetable Samosas, 32
    Mixed Vegetable Curry, 37
    Mushy Peas, 85
    Onion Bhajis, 31
    Quick Vegetable Stir-fry, 50
    Roasted Corn Cobs, 109
    Root Crisps, 97
    Sag Aloo, 35
    Spring Rolls, 62
    Szechuan Spicy Peanut Noodles with
        Vegetables, 58
    Thai Red Vegetable Curry, 135
    Vegetable Shish Kebabs, 129
    Vegetable Tempura, 151
    Veggie Burgers, 94
    See also potatoes, salads
Village Salad, 131

What's in My Fridge Stuffed Pizza, 75
Wonton Soup, 47